CR~~...~~
SUGARPASTE

STEPHEN BENISON

MEREHURST

To Karina, for your constant help and support.
To Laura and Ashley, for your patience and understanding.

≈

Published in 1994 by Merehurst Limited, Ferry House,
51–57 Lacy Road, Putney, London SW15 1PR

ISBN 1 85391 350 2

Managing Editor Bridget Jones
Edited by Liz Godfray
Designed by Jo Tapper
Photography by Sue Atkinson
Colour separation by Fotographics Limited, UK-Hong Kong
Printed by Wing King Tong, Hong Kong

Acknowledgements
Special thanks to Clarice Tadd and Stuart Simpson.
The author and publishers would like to thank the following for their assistance.
A Piece Of Cake, 18 Upper High Street, Tame, Oxon, OX9 3EX.
Cake Art Ltd, Venture Way, Crown Estate, Priors Wood, Taunton, Somerset TA2 8DE.
J.F Renshaw Ltd, (for Regalice used for covering the cakes), Crown Street, Liverpool,
L8 7RF (UK)
Orchard Products, 49 Langdale Road, Hove, E. Sussex BN3 4HR.
P.M.E (Harrow) Ltd, Sugarcraft Division, Brember Road, S. Harrow, Middx., HA2 8UN.
Squires Kitchen, Squires House, 3 Waverley Lane, Farnham, Surrey GU9 8BB.

NOTES ON USING THE RECIPES
For all recipes, quantities are given in metric, Imperial and cup
measurements. Follow one set of measures only as they are not
interchangeable. Standard 5ml teaspoons (tsp) and 15ml tablespoons
(tbsp) are used. Australian readers, whose tablespoons measure 20ml,
should adjust quantities accordingly. All spoon measures are assumed to
be level unless otherwise stated.
Eggs are a standard size 3 (medium) unless otherwise stated.

CONTENTS

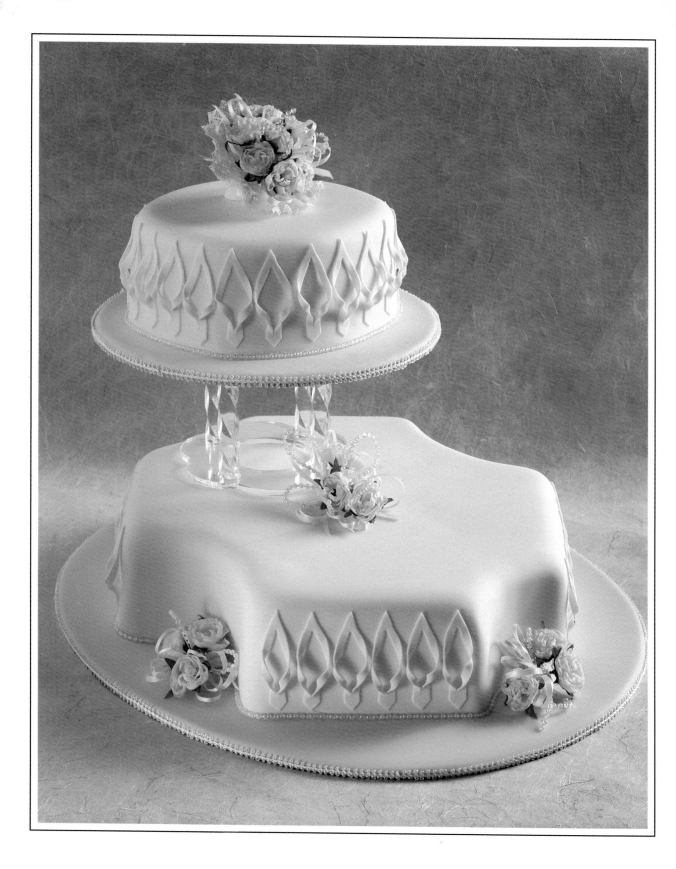

INTRODUCTION

Sugarpaste has become a widely popular cake decorating medium, particularly over the last decade. The many different uses and techniques to which it can be applied are endless. Creative Sugarpaste shows the basic skills and techniques which will enable the beginner, with a little practice, to achieve a rewarding and impressive end result.

Following the chapter of basic techniques, each of the cake designs featured on the pages which follow illustrates a specific skill. The skills and designs may be interchanged according to personal choice and your requirements for the occasion. Even though you may only have a limited range of cake decorating equipment, it is still worth experimenting on spare pieces of sugarpaste to discover different ways of using the tools. An item which you anticipated using simply for one design can sometimes be adapted to apply an alternative effect. When working with as versatile a medium as sugarpaste there are many skills which can be borrowed from other crafts – but always remember that you are working with a food item which will be eaten!

One example of my experiments with sugarpaste is included in this book: the idea for the link twist design developed when I was twisting cut-out pieces of sugarpaste. I left them to dry and coloured the twisted section, then placed them together and was pleased with the refreshing effect for a side decoration. It is in this way that many of the techniques shown have evolved through the innovations of keen cake decorators and the wider availability of the various pieces of equipment. I have also introduced some different techniques which I hope you will enjoy trying. Whether you are new to cake decorating or looking for unusual and different ideas, perhaps one of the skills shown here will give you the inspiration to try and create your own special cake decoration.

RICH FRUIT CAKE

❖

You can use your own favourite recipe, or try this moist rich fruit cake.

	Diameter using round cake tin				
	15cm (6 in)	18cm (7 in)	20cm (8 in)	23cm (9 in)	25cm (10 in)
dried fruit	500g (1 lb)	750g (1½ lb)	1kg (2 lb)	1.25kg(2½ lb)	1.5kg (3 lb)
stout beer	2 tbsp	3 tbsp	4 tbsp	5 tbsp	6 tbsp
butter	125g (4 oz/½ cup)	185g (6 oz/¾ cup)	250g (8 oz/1 cup)	315g (10 oz/1¼ cups)	375g (12 oz/1½ cups)
caster (superfine) sugar	125g (4 oz/½ cup)	185g (6 oz/¾ cup)	250g (8 oz/1 cup)	315g (10 oz/1¼ cups)	375g (12 oz/1½ cups)
black treacle (molasses)	2 tsp	3 tsp	5 tsp	6 tsp	8 tsp
glacé (candied) cherries	15g (½ oz/1 tbsp)	30g (1 oz/2 tbsp)	60g (2 oz/⅓ cup)	75g (2½ oz/5 tbsp)	90g (3 oz/½ cup)
plain (all-purpose) flour	155g (5 oz/1¼ cups)	220g (7 oz/1¾ cups)	280g (9 oz/2¼ cups)	345g (11 oz/2¾ cups)	410g (13 oz/3¼ cups)
eggs, medium	2	3	4	5	6
ground mixed spice (apple pie spice)	¼ tsp	½ tsp	1 tsp	1½ tsp	2 tsp
cocoa (unsweetened cocoa powder)	1 tsp	1½ tsp	2 tsp	2½ tsp	3 tsp
ground almonds	15g (½ oz/2 tbsp)	30g (1 oz/¼ cup)	60g (2 oz/½ cup)	75g (2½ oz/⅔ cup)	90g (3 oz/¾ cup)
candied peel (optional)	60g (2 oz/⅓ cup)	125g (4 oz/¾ cup)	155g (5 oz/1 cup)	185g (6 oz/1 cup)	250g (8 oz/1½ cups)

NOTES

Cake Sizes For a 15cm(6 in) square cake use the 18cm(7 in) recipe quantities. For a 30cm(12 in) round cake make one and a half times the recipe for the 25cm(10 in) cake, and one and three-quarters times for a 30cm(12 in) square.

Varying the Fruit If preferred, instead of candied peel, add the grated rind of ½ orange and ½ lemon. Dried fruit, such as currants, sultanas, white raisins and raisins can be used, with a higher proportion of currants giving best results. Rinse fruit in hot water to plump it up. Drain, dry and soak in the beer overnight.

Grease and line the tin (pan) with non-stick paper. Preheat oven to 150°C(300°F/Gas 2).

Cream the butter and sugar until light and creamy. Add the black treacle.

Wash and dry the cherries, then cut into quarters. Dust with a little of the flour.

Beat the eggs, then gradually beat them into the butter and sugar mixture. Sift in flour, spices, cocoa and ground almonds.

Fold in the dried fruit and candied peel, and place in the prepared tin.

Secure a double thickness of brown paper around the outside of the tin to prevent the edge of the cake from burning.

Cook in the preheated oven for 1 hour, then reduce the temperature to 120°C (250°F/ Gas ½). Continue to cook according to the size of the cake: a further 1 hour for 15cm(6 in), 1½ hours for 18cm(7 in), 2¼ hours for 20cm(8 in), 3 hours for 23cm(9 in) and 3¾ hours for 25cm (10 in). A tray of water placed on the bottom of the oven will assist in the baking. To test if the cake is cooked, insert a metal skewer into the centre; it should come out clean.

Allow cake to cool in the tin for a while, then transfer to a wire rack. When cooled sprinkle with 2 – 4 tablespoons of brandy over a period of 4 days. Wrap in greaseproof paper (parchment) and place in a polythene bag. Do not seal the bag tightly, but allow the cake to 'breathe'. Store until ready to decorate.

MARZIPAN (ALMOND PASTE)

❖

COATING WITH MARZIPAN (ALMOND PASTE) To calculate the amount of marzipan needed, weigh the cake and use half the total weight. For example, a cake weighing 2kg(4 lb) would need 1kg(2 lb) marzipan.

~ 1 ~

Trim surface of cake if uneven. Fill any small holes and indents with marzipan (almond paste). Turn cake over so that the bottom faces up. Fill any gap around the bottom edge of cake with marzipan. Place on parchment and brush with hot apricot glaze.

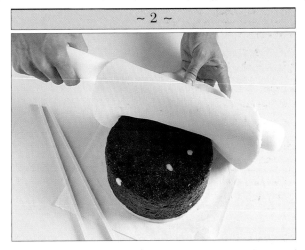

~ 2 ~

Knead the marzipan (almond paste) until pliable on a surface lightly dusted with icing (confectioners') sugar. Roll out between spacers, then polish with a smoother. Lift over the cake with the rolling pin. Mould onto the cake by hand. Trim and polish with a smoother.

EXPERT ADVICE

≈

It is particularly important to achieve an even finish on the marzipan coating. Failure to ensure the surface is smooth will result in an uneven surface onto which to apply the sugarpaste.

SUGARPASTE COVERING

❖

There are many different manufactured sugarpastes on the market, each producing pleasing results. Before these became widely available a home-made paste was used which required a lot of arm muscle! The recipe given was the one I first used, flavoured with lemon essence to take the sweetness off the paste.

Today, not only can you buy ready-made pastes but they are also available in a wide variety of colours. When opening the packet of sugarpaste it is important to work it until soft and pliable; a little icing (confectioners') sugar dusted on the work surface will prevent the paste from sticking. Important items of equipment include a non-stick rolling pin, long enough to cover the required width of the paste, and smoothers to give a silky smooth finish. The use of spacers will enable you to achieve an even thickness on all coverings.

1kg (2 lb/6 cups) icing (confectioners') sugar
4 tsp powdered gelatine
4 tbsp cold water
125ml (4 fl oz/½ cup) liquid glucose (clear corn syrup)
1 – 2 tsp glycerine
4 drops of lemon essence (extract)

Sift the icing sugar into a bowl. Sprinkle the gelatine onto the cold water in a small bowl. Leave to soften for 3 – 4 minutes, until sponged. Stand the bowl over a saucepan of hot (not boiling) water and stir the gelatine until dissolved. Warm the liquid glucose and glycerine in a small saucepan over gentle heat. In damp weather use only one teaspoon glycerine; when conditions are dry increase this to two. Add all the liquids and lemon essence to the icing sugar and stir until the mixture starts to bind together. Turn out onto a surface lightly dusted with icing sugar and knead until the paste is smooth and pliable. Store in an airtight polythene bag and knead well again before using.

NOTE Glycerine is a hygroscopic agent. This means it attracts moisture and keeps the paste soft. It is added to the sugarpaste in varying quantities, depending on the humidity of the atmosphere.

EXPERT ADVICE

≈

Do not use cornflour (cornstarch) for rolling out sugarpaste as the natural yeast in the flour will start to ferment with the sugar on the surface of the marzipan (almond paste) or cake.

~ 1 ~

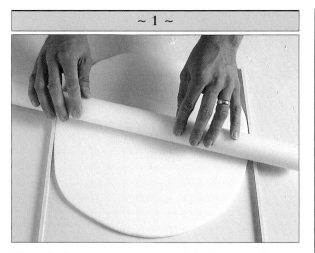

Knead the sugarpaste until it is smooth and pliable, then lightly dust the work surface with icing (confectioners') sugar. Place the spacers on either side of the sugarpaste, then gently roll away from yourself. Roll the paste slightly larger than the top and sides of the cake.

~ 2 ~

Brush the cake with clear alcohol. Lift the sugarpaste over the cake on the rolling pin. Smooth by hand from the cake top down the sides. Avoid trapping air bubbles; these can be punctured with a clean sharp point then polished.

~ 3 ~

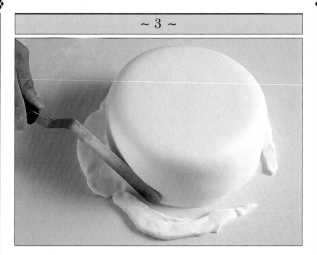

Trim the surplus paste around the base of the cake with a palette knife, holding it parallel to the side as you cut. Place the cake on a piece of parchment. Do not use any excess icing (confectioners') sugar on the cake as it will not give a satin smooth finish.

~ 4 ~

Take a smoother and position it upright against the side of the cake. Apply even pressure and gently rotate the smoother around the cake edge until a smooth and even surface is achieved. Polish the top of the cake with the smoother and the curved edge with the palm of your hand.

~ ❖ ~

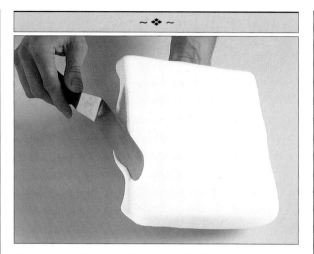

ONE-PIECE BOARD COVERING *Roll the sugarpaste 5mm(¼ in) thick and brush the board with clear alcohol, taking care not to splash the paste. Unroll the paste from the rolling pin over the board. Trim excess and smooth edge and top with smoothers. Allow to dry.*

~ ❖ ~

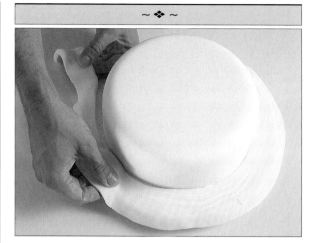

STRIP BOARD COVERING *Roll a strip of sugarpaste to go around the cake. Cut a straight edge on one side. Brush the board with clear alcohol. Place the cut paste edge against the cake; trim excess. Cut the paste and join the ends, then polish with smoothers.*

~ ❖ ~

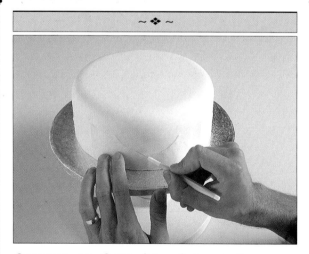

SCRIBING ON CAKE SIDE *Cut out the paper template and position around the cake, securing in place with a little sticky tape. Use a scriber to mark the outline of the paper template, then remove.*

~ ❖ ~

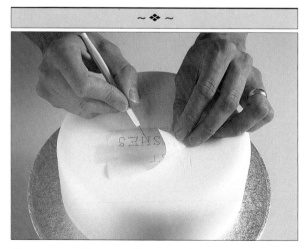

SCRIBING WORDS *Trace the message onto parchment and secure to the dry sugarpaste covering with a little sticky tape. Use the scriber and press gently over the message. Remove the paper and pipe over the message with a no.1 piping tube (tip) and soft royal icing.*

COVERING THE CAKE BOARD IN ONE PIECE

❖

Roll the sugarpaste 5mm(¼ in) thick. Brush the cake board with clear alcohol. Take care not to splash the sugarpaste as the alcohol will leave a mark on it. Secure the paste to the board. Trim the excess paste around the edge of the board with a palette knife, cutting with a downwards action. Take care not to stretch the paste as you cut it. Smooth the top and edges with smoothers, then allow the paste to dry before putting the cake on the board.

COVERING THE CAKE BOARD BY THE STRIP METHOD

❖

The strip method of covering the board edge uses less sugarpaste and can be applied to both round and shaped cakes. A strip of paste is applied to the board around the cake, placing it up to the cake edge and trimming excess paste. Smooth the joins in the paste together with a circular motion using the first two fingers, then polish it with smoothers. Place a piece of parchment cut to the exact size of the cake between the cake and the foil board covering to prevent the acid in the fruit cake from reacting with the foil. This is particularly important if the cake is to be stored for a long period of time, such as one tier of a wedding cake.

SCRIBING A DESIGN

❖

The paper template is secured to the surface of the cake with sticky tape.

When scribing around the edge of the template, hold the scriber at a 45° angle to the cake surface. Take care not to press too hard on the scriber or you will cut into the sugarpaste covering instead of simply marking its surface. When the design has been scribed on the cake side, as shown left, the mark may be used as a guide for applying a frill to the cake or for attaching other decoration as well as for piping.

SCRIBING WORDS

❖

Trace the message onto parchment and secure it to the dry sugarpaste covering. Carefully scribe over the message with a scriber, to imprint the message onto the sugarpaste. Remove the paper and pipe over the imprint with soft royal icing. White royal icing can be piped first, then a coloured icing piped on top.

DECORATIVE TECHNIQUES

~ ❖ ~

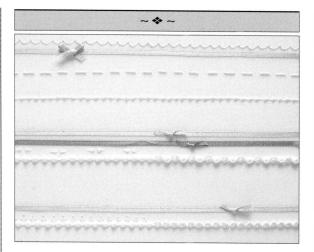

~ ❖ ~

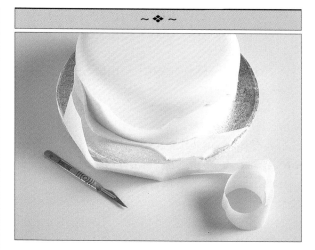

BEADWORK *Holding the piping tube (tip) at a 45° angle to the cake and piping towards yourself will help to create even-sized beads. The amount of pressure applied and the consistency of the icing is important.*

DRAPE *Dry base coat for 2 days. Roll out sugarpaste to 3mm(⅛ in) thick. Brush only the top edge of the cake with alcohol. Lay the paste on top, position the template and cut the drape with a scalpel. Pipe royal icing beads around the drape edge with a no.1 piping tube (tip).*

~ ❖ ~

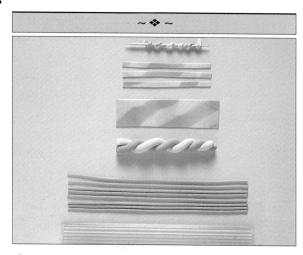

~ ❖ ~

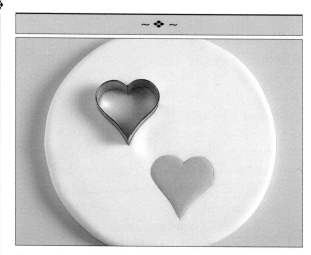

GARLANDS *Roll frill paste thinly and cut out with the plastic cutter; secure to cake with sugar glue. Twist two colours of paste together, roll thinly and cut into strips. Twist a strip around a cocktail stick (toothpick) and secure to cake. Then remove the cocktail stick.*

INLAY *Stamp out the required shape in the soft sugarpaste. Do not cut down into the marzipan (almond paste). Remove the shape while the cutter is still in place and leave the sugarpaste covering to dry. Insert coloured paste cut to the same shape; smooth surface with smoothers.*

BEAD WORK AND RIBBON FINISH

❖

Place about 1½ tablespoons royal icing onto a side scraper or flat surface. With a small palette knife, paddle the icing backwards and forwards to remove any air bubbles. Liquid or paste colour should be added at this stage and blended until even. Fit a plain piping tube (tip) into a piping bag and fill with the icing, then pipe beads around the base of the cake.

A ribbon placed above the bead work around the base of the cake, or below piped decorations, adds colour and interest to the design. Secure ribbon to the cake surface with sugar glue or small dots of soft royal icing. Placing a small bow on the ribbon ends will conceal the join.

APPLY A DRAPE

❖

Cover the cake with sugarpaste as shown on page 9. Allow to dry for 2 days. Roll sugarpaste 3mm(⅛ in) thick and then brush just the top edge of the cake with alcohol. Place the sugarpaste drape over the cake and smooth to form the cake shape. Trim surplus paste around the base of the cake then place the paper template around the cake. Cut out the shape with a scalpel, taking care not to cut into the dry cake covering. Embossing decoration can be applied to the drape edge while the paste is still soft. Pipe small beads of royal icing with a no. 1 piping tube (tip) around the edge of the drape to finish it off neatly.

INLAY TECHNIQUE

❖

Cover the cake with marzipan (almond paste) and sugarpaste. While the paste is still soft, mark the position and cut out the required shape for the inlay section. Take care to cut only the sugarpaste and not down into the marzipan. Leaving the cutter in place, use the point of a dresden tool to lift out the sugarpaste shape. Remove the cutter and leave the sugarpaste coating to dry. Roll out coloured paste to the same thickness as the sugarpaste covering on the cake. Stamp out a coloured shape and insert this in place in the cut-out section on the cake. Smooth over the top with smoothers to flatten the inlay section neatly into place.

ROYAL ICING

❖

22g (¾ oz/9 tsp) albumen powder
155ml (5 fl oz/⅔ cup) warm water
875g (1¾ lb/5¼ cups) icing (confectioners')
sugar, sifted

◉ Mix albumen powder with warm water and allow to stand for 15 minutes. Strain into a grease-free bowl, add two-thirds of the icing sugar and beat on slow speed with an electric mixer for 3 minutes. Add the remaining icing sugar and continue to beat for a further 2 minutes, until the icing stands in a soft peak and appears glossy. Adjust the consistency with a little water when required for writing and bead work.

CRIMPER WORK

Crimper work is fairly simple to do but a few helpful tips will ensure a successful result. Make sure the crimper jaw is free from any soft sugarpaste before inserting into the cake covering. Do not have the jaw and the angle by which you insert the crimper too wide. Have the cake tilted slightly away from you and hold the crimper at right angles to the cake surface when in use. Practise on a spare piece of paste before you start on the cake.

EMBOSSING

There are numerous embossing stamps available, ranging from specially manufactured tools to the use of buttons, modelling tools and even elaborate spoon handles. Many of the plastic cake ornaments available can also be used to emboss the paste. Colour the embossed design when dry with diluted food colouring, taking care not to have too much moisture on the brush when applying the colour to the paste. Dilute the food colouring with alcohol as this dries more quickly than water.

MAKING AN EMBOSSING STAMP

The step, right, shows how to make an embossing stamp or embosser. This allows any chosen design to be imprinted in soft sugarpaste. The home-made embosser can be used up to 20 – 30 times – sometimes longer – if treated carefully. Names and messages can be made using this method but they must be traced in reverse image onto the perspex (plexiglass) so that the embossed impression comes out the right way.

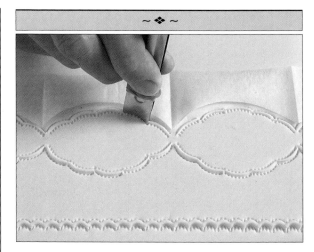

CRIMPER WORK Place template on soft paste. Place an elastic band around the crimper to set the jaws 1cm(½ in) apart. Dust the jaws with icing (confectioners') sugar and push into the paste, just above template, pinching together as you insert. Repeat around the side of the cake.

EMBOSSING The embossing stamp must be clean and free from any dry icing (confectioners') sugar. Hold the embosser firmly and apply even pressure into the soft sugarpaste. Avoid rocking the embosser from side to side as this will distort the impression.

Best Wishes, see page 64

*Design for making embossing stamp
Mirror image for piping*

Design when embossed in paste

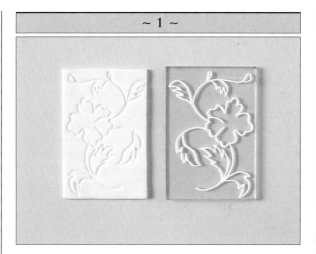

MAKING AN EMBOSSER *Place the chosen design under a small piece of perspex (plexiglass) and pipe over the outline with a no.1 piping tube (tip) and white royal icing. Allow to dry for 3 – 4 hours before using.*

USING A HOME-MADE EMBOSSER *Place the embosser design on sugarpaste. Apply even pressure on the back of the perspex (plexiglass), then carefully remove to mark design on sugar. Cut out while soft and apply to the cake. When dry, paint with diluted food colour.*

~ ❖ ~

FRILL *Roll the frill paste thinly and cut out using the frill cutter. Position the cocktail stick (toothpick) on the edge of the frill and gently roll it while applying forwards pressure. A little cornflour (cornstarch) on the board will prevent the paste from sticking.*

~ ❖ ~

FLOUNCE *This is a more emphasized frill. Roll the frill paste thinly and cut out with the frill cutter. Position the cocktail stick (toothpick) on the edge of the frill. This time roll backwards and forwards, applying even pressure. Cut in half to apply to the cake, see page 24.*

~ ❖ ~

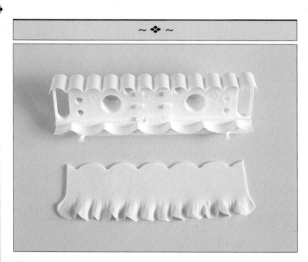

ENDLESS FRILL CUTTER *Roll out the frill paste thinly into a rectangle. Place the cutter onto the paste and push down firmly. Frill the edge of the paste as for the flounce and then apply to the cake with sugar glue.*

~ ❖ ~

RIBBON INSERTION *Work the flower paste until it is soft and pliable then roll out on a board lightly greased with white vegetable fat (shortening). Use a scalpel and a ruler to cut strips of paste 1cm (½ in) long by 5mm (¼ in) wide. Dry over a lightly greased wooden dowel.*

FRILL

The frilled edge on the paste is created by applying even forwards pressure while rolling the edge of the paste gently with a cocktail stick (toothpick). If the paste starts to crack on the edge, work a little white vegetable fat (shortening) into it and roll it out again.

FLOUNCE

A flounce has a more delicate and fuller appearance than a frill. To achieve more movement in the frilled edge, a backwards and forwards rolling action is applied with the edge of the cocktail stick (toothpick).

ENDLESS FRILL CUTTER

The endless frill cutter can be used to achieve a minimum of joins around the side of the cake. Roll out the frill paste into a thin strip and then stamp out the length required, frilling the scalloped edge as shown on the flounce.

RIBBON INSERTION

This is the use of flower paste, cut into short strips to represent threaded ribbon. The pieces of paste are dried over dowelling so that they set in a curved shape. They are then inserted into slits cut in the cake covering as shown on page 24.

The coating on the cake should be partly dried but not completely set before the ribbon insertion technique is used.

FLOWER PASTE

Flower paste is used extensively in cake decorating, particularly for moulding sugar flowers. It can also be used for small plaques and decorations to complement the cake. Each cake decorator will have his or her own preferred paste but this quick and simple recipe will enable you to produce the items shown in this book and to experiment further.

 Make the royal icing as shown on page 13. Carefully measure 250g (8 oz/½ lb) royal icing and add 15g (½ oz/16 tsp) of Tylose powder (carboxymethyl cellulose). The paste will thicken. Turn it out onto a board and knead a little cornflour (cornstarch) and white vegetable fat (shortening) into the paste. Knead until the paste is stretchy and it makes a clicking sound. Place in a polythene bag and keep in an airtight container in the refrigerator to rest for 12 hours before use.

FRILL PASTE

Whereas sugarpaste is too soft for some techniques, without sufficient hold to achieve the required effect, flower paste sets too hard. Frill paste can be made by combining equal amounts of flower paste and sugarpaste to give a more versatile paste than either flower paste or sugarpaste.

By using frill paste you will be able to achieve a finer finish. This mixture of pastes is also known as modelling paste.

~ ❖ ~

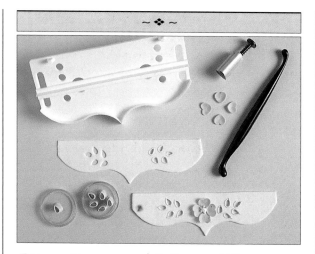

EYELET EMBROIDERY *Roll out frill paste to 1mm(1/32 in) thick and stamp out the shape. Use an eyelet cutter to stamp out eyelet holes. Secure to the cake with sugar glue, then pipe around the holes with soft royal icing and a no.1 piping tube (tip). Flowers may be added.*

~ ❖ ~

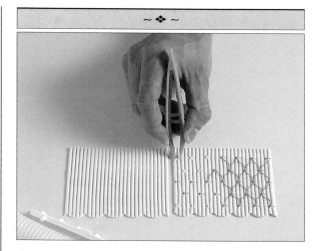

SMOCKING *Roll out paste to 3mm(1/8 in) thick; roll with ribbed roller. Scallop the edges with the endless frill cutter. Secure to cake with sugar glue. Pinch alternate pairs of ribs with tweezers, working across in required pattern. Use a no.1 piping tube (tip), to pipe 'stitches'.*

~ ❖ ~

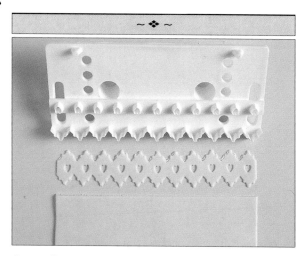

LACE CUTTERS *Knead the frill paste, roll out to 1mm(1/16 in) thick and cut using the lace cutter with the small heart insert. Remove heart insert and cut the other paste edge to make the lace. Scribe a line on the cake; tilt cake slightly away from you and secure the lace with sugar glue.*

~ ❖ ~

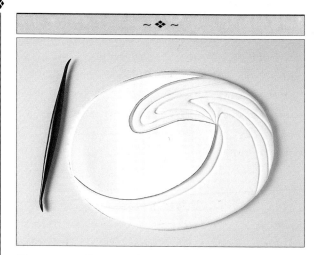

EMBOSSED SPIRAL *Cut out section of enlarged template on broken lines. Place on soft paste and use to mark first section with side of dresden tool. Remove template; mark remaining spirals freehand, allowing 1cm(1/2 in) space between each and working down cake to board.*

SUGAR GLUE

❖

Sugar glue is used to stick sugar pieces together. In a small saucepan, heat together 125g(4 oz/ ¼ lb) sugarpaste and 2 tablespoons water, then boil until clear. Store in an airtight container in the refrigerator until required. Other glues such as egg white and gum arabic solution can be used instead of sugar glue.

EYELET EMBROIDERY

❖

The eyelet embroidery shown left can be repeated without having too many joins between. Roll out the frill paste and then cut two adjoining sections with the open-ended cutter. Cut out the eyelet holes with the eyelet cutter, then secure the shape to the cake side with sugar glue.

Pipe around each of the eyelet holes with soft royal icing. Small hearts which have been cut out in coloured flower paste are secured to the side of the cake with royal icing to form the flower shape, in the centre of the eyelet embroidery. The heart-shaped engagement cake pictured on page 43 has been decorated using this technique.

SMOCKING

❖

Use the Smocking Paste, right, for this technique. If you are working on a round cake, or you want the smocking to continue around the cake without a break, cut the necessary number of paste pieces and apply them to the cake side at the desired height. Then begin to work the design, pinching the ribs together as shown in the step picture. When the design is pinched into the paste all around the cake, pipe over the ribs which are pinched together. This forms the smocking effect and highlights the shape of the design.

SMOCKING PASTE

❖

250g (8 oz/½ lb) sugarpaste
1 tsp Tylose (carboxymethyl cellulose) or
gum tragacanth powder

● Knead the sugarpaste until it is soft and pliable and then work in the Tylose or gum tragacanth powder. Store in an airtight polythene bag until required.

LACE CUTTERS

❖

The use of frill paste for the cut out lace will create a light and delicate effect on the finished cake. The paste can be rolled and the open-ended cutter applied repeatedly along its length to give long strips of lace which will go around the cake without too many joins.

CORNFLOUR (CORNSTARCH) DUSTING BAG

❖

Cut a circle of muslin (cheesecloth) or fine cotton material measuring about 18cm (6 in) in diameter. Place some cornflour (cornstarch) in the middle and gather the fabric around it to make a neat bundle. Secure the fabric with an elastic band. Use this when rolling out frill or flower paste.

~ ❖ ~

LACE *Place acetate film or waxed paper over perspex (plexiglass). Trace design five times on paper longer than acetate. Lightly grease acetate with white vegetable fat (shortening). Pipe over design with a no.0 piping tube (tip) and royal icing. Slide template and repeat.*

~ ❖ ~

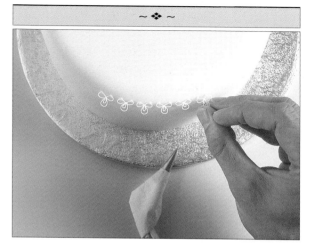

APPLYING LACE *Carefully remove the piped lace using a cranked palette knife, and place on a piece of sponge. With a no.0 piping tube (tip) and white royal icing, pipe two small dots on the cake. Pick up a lace piece and secure to the royal icing using thumb and index finger.*

~ ❖ ~

BLOSSOM CUTTER FLOWERS *Stamp out blossom. Place on foam and use ball tool to flute edges. Place blossom in a small ring of paste. Pipe soft royal icing in centre; sprinkle with coloured semolina. Pipe small coloured stamens. Tint petal edges with liquid colouring.*

~ ❖ ~

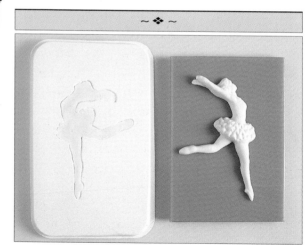

USING MOULDS *Colour the sugarpaste a flesh colour. Ensure the paste is free from any small cracks. Lightly dust with cornflour (cornstarch) and push into the mould. Trim off excess paste. Loosen from mould edge and turn out; leave to dry. Paint detail with diluted food colouring.*

PIPED LACE

❖

The design is traced on paper which is long enough to pull from side to side under the perspex - this allows the paper to be moved along after each set of traced lace is piped. Use a small piping bag and a no.0 piping tube (tip) for finer results. A no.1 piping tube (tip) can be used but a heavier looking lace will be produced. Ensure the royal icing is paddled on a side scraper or flat surface with a small palette knife to remove any small air bubbles before filling the piping bag. Dry the lace under an anglepoise lamp for quicker results. If the piping tube becomes blocked place the end of the tube in a little boiling water to clear; never force any sharp object into the tube end.

APPLYING LACE

❖

Following the curve of the top edge of the cake, or above the top of a frill, pipe small dots of royal icing onto the cake surface. Then attach each lace piece carefully using thumb and index finger, not tweezers. Ensure the angle of the applied lace is consistent. Leave to dry. While you are still developing basic skills you are less likely to break the lace by leaving a gap between each piece. When you are more confident, the lace pieces should be applied closer together so that they are more or less touching.

BLOSSOM CUTTER FLOWERS

❖

Ensure the flower paste is rolled thinly before stamping out the petal shape. Flute the edges of each petal with the ball tool on a piece of foam or sponge, then cup the centre. Place the blossom in a small ring of paste and pipe a ball of soft royal icing in the centre. Allow to dry then sprinkle with coloured semolina. Pipe two rings of stamens using a no.1 piping tube (tip) with coloured royal icing and finally tint the edges of the petals with liquid food colouring.

USING MOULDS

❖

Have the approximate amount of sugarpaste to press into the mould kneaded and smooth on the surface. Lightly dust the paste with cornflour and press it into the mould. Then excess paste can be removed with a small cranked palette knife. Loosen the edges of the paste from around the mould and turn the model out. Use a scalpel and cut the paste to create details, such as the hands on the ballet dancer. Position the model on a flat surface to dry. Use diluted food colourings to paint in the detail and then secure the model to the cake surface with a little sugar glue.

A CHRISTENING

20cm(8 in) round cake
apricot glaze
750g(1½ lb) marzipan (almond paste)
1kg(2 lb) white sugarpaste
lemon yellow paste food colour
clear alcohol (gin, vodka, kirsch)
50 pieces of sugar ribbon insertion, see page 16
egg white or Sugar Glue, see page 19
small amount of Royal Icing, see page 13
125g(4 oz/¼ lb) Frill Paste, see page 17
lemon yellow dusting powder
(petal dust/blossom tint)
cornflour (cornstarch)
2 sugar daisies, see page 33
FOR THE ROCKING HORSE
155g(5 oz) Flower Paste, see page 17
chestnut brown, black and daffodil yellow
liquid food colourings
white vegetable fat (shortening)
light brown dusting powder (petal dust/blossom tint)
EQUIPMENT
ribbon insertion cutter ● medium paintbrush
28cm(11 in) thick round cake board
no. 1, 2 and 3 piping tubes (tips)
small rolling pin and board ● scalpel
drying board ● foam or sponge pad ● scriber
1m(1 yd) of 1cm(½ in) wide yellow ribbon

Brush cake with apricot glaze and then cover with marzipan. Allow to dry. Colour the sugarpaste pale lemon to create the marble effect. Brush cake with alcohol and then cover as shown on page 9.

Measure the circumference of the cake and cut a band of parchment to fit around it exactly. Fold the paper into eight equal sections. Trace the design on page 66 onto the folded paper and cut out. Open out the band of paper and secure it around the cake with a little sticky tape.

Mark the slots for the ribbon insertion as in step 3 on page 24, following the spacing marks on the paper quite carefully as you work. Brush each length of ribbon at both ends with a little egg white or sugar glue, then insert the ends into the cuts in the sugarpaste covering.

Carefully place the cake on the board. Use a no. 2 piping tube and white royal icing to pipe beads around the base of the cake. Leave to dry.

Use a small board and rolling pin to roll out the frill paste and cut out, see page 16. Attach frill to cake following step 4 on page 24. Use a no. 1 piping tube and white royal icing to pipe the decoration between the ribbon insertion. Dust the frill with lemon yellow colour.

Make the rocking horse following the instructions on page 25. To complete the cake, scribe the message on the sugarpaste as shown on page 10. Use a no. 1 piping tube and white royal icing to pipe the message. Attach the rocking horse with a small bulb of royal icing. Finally attach the daisies with a little royal icing and trim the board edge with ribbon to complete.

EXPERT ADVICE
≈

Use a soft, medium flat brush to apply dusting powder to the frill and place a piece of tissue paper underneath to catch the surplus colour. To lighten the colour of dusting powder, mix it with a little cornflour (cornstarch).

~ 1 ~

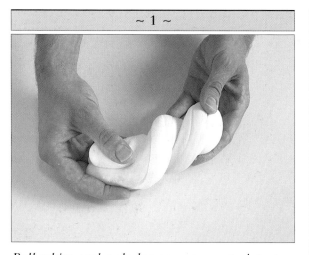

Roll white and pale lemon sugarpaste into two separate sausage shapes, then twist together. Fold the twist back on itself to combine the two colours and give a marbled effect. Do not overwork the paste.

~ 2 ~

Roll out frill paste and cut out with the frill cutter. Position the grooved plastic frill roller on the edge of the paste and apply pressure as you roll it forward to frill and mark the paste.

~ 3 ~

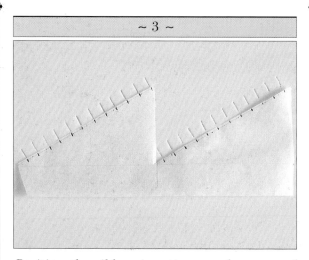

Position the ribbon insertion template around the cake. Following the marks, cut into the paste using a ribbon insertion cutter or scalpel. Remove template.

~ 4 ~

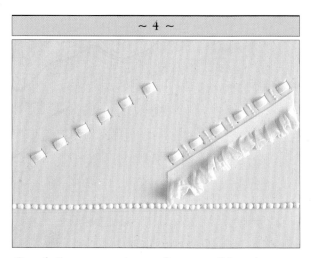

Carefully secure pieces of sugar ribbon into cut slits with sugar glue. Attach the textured frill and pipe between the pieces.

~ 1 ~

ROCKING HORSE *Trace template onto paper and cut out. Roll out 140g (4½ oz) light brown flower paste 5mm(¼ in) thick. Lightly rub template back with vegetable fat and place on paste. Use scalpel to cut out horse, remove template and dry for 24 hours, turning at intervals.*

~ 2 ~

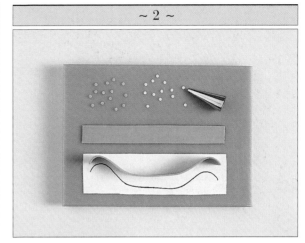

Cut out 10 light brown circles using the end of a no.3 piping tube (tip). Darken the paste with brown colour. Roll out 5mm(¼ in) thick and cut out the base. Position it to dry on the side edge over the curved template. Using a little pale lemon flower paste, cut out 10 more circles.

~ 3 ~

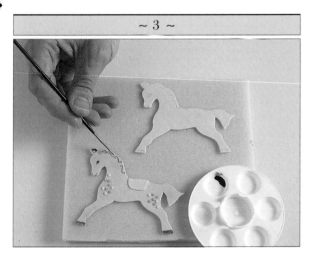

Place saddle template on pale lemon paste and cut out with a scalpel. Secure to horse with sugar glue. Trace and paint details, using black food colouring for eye. Repeat on the other side. Apply light brown dusting powder for shading. Secure small paste circles with sugar glue.

~ 4 ~

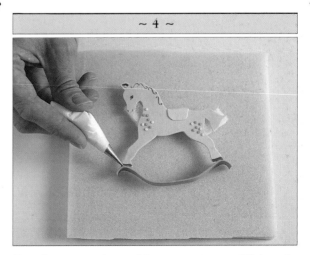

Lay horse on piece of foam or sponge. With pale brown royal icing and no.1 piping tube (tip), secure the base to the hooves of the horse and allow to dry. With a no.1 piping tube (tip) and white royal icing, pipe a line from the nostril to the saddle on both sides.

ELIZABETHAN WEDDING CAKE

30cm(10 in) square cake
apricot glaze
1.5kg(3 lb) marzipan (almond paste)
2.25kg(4½ lb) white sugarpaste
clear alcohol (gin, vodka, kirsch)
old gold/yellow liquid food colouring
small amount of Royal Icing, see page 13
185g(6 oz) Frill Paste, see page 17
Sugar Glue, see page 19
yellow dusting powder (petal dust/blossom tint)

EQUIPMENT

38cm(15 in) thin oval cake board
20cm(8 in) thin round cake board
4m(4½ yd) pearl beading
diamond link twist cutter
dresden modelling tool
ribbon insertion cutter
soft medium paintbrush
22 pale yellow silk roses
3m(3¼ yd) of 3mm(⅛ in) wide lemon ribbon
white stem fix ● white posy frill
2m(2¼ yd) thin white brocade
perspex (plexiglass) separators

Cut out the paper templates and place them onto the cake. Take a small sharp knife and, holding it in an upright position, cut around the paper templates. Assemble the cut pieces to make the smaller cake as shown in the diagram on page 29. This cake will require a little apricot glaze between the cut sections to secure them together. Brush both cakes with apricot glaze and cover with marzipan, following the instructions on page 7. Allow to dry.

Cover both the cakes with 1.5kg(3 lb) white sugarpaste, brushing first with clear alcohol, and set aside to dry. Colour the remaining paste an old gold/yellow and cover the cake boards in one piece as shown on page 10. Allow to dry.

Position the cakes carefully onto the covered boards and secure the pearl beading around the base of the cakes with white royal icing.

Roll out the frill paste to 1mm(⅟₁₆ in) thick and cut out with the diamond link twist cutter, to make 46 pieces. Feed the long pointed end through the centre cut, creating a twist, and secure to the side of the cake with sugar glue. Trim the top of each link twist with the edge of the ribbon insertion cutter to neaten. Continue around the larger cake, applying the link twist effect on the straight sides, and then repeat all around the small cake.

When the link twist is dry, take yellow dusting powder and a soft medium paintbrush to apply colour to the twisted section.

Make five sprays of yellow silk roses, adding ribbon loops and pearl beading. Make a posy using a bought posy frill to hold the silk flowers. Place the sprays of flowers and the small posy onto the cakes, securing them in place with small pieces of white sugarpaste.

Trim the edge of the boards with white brocade and assemble the cake with the perspex (plexiglass) separators.

NOTE Ensure that the beading is removed from the cake before it is cut.

EXPERT ADVICE

≈

After placing the cake on the covered board, fill any small gaps between the cake and the board with white royal icing. Remove any excess with a small palette knife.

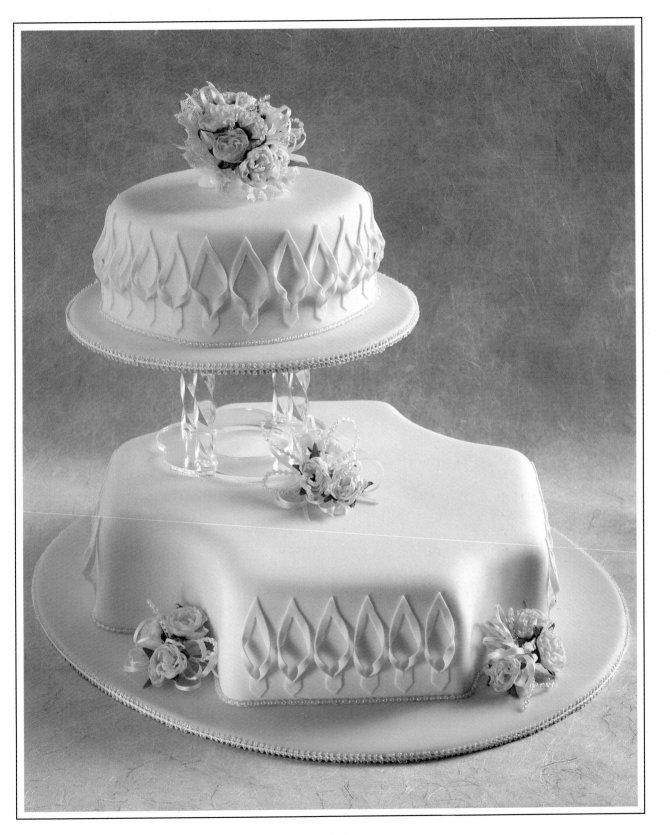

~ 1 ~

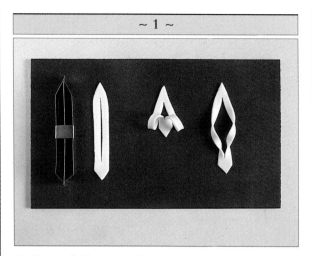

Roll out frill paste thinly and cut with the link twist cutter, taking care to press firmly and give a clean cut to the edge of the paste. Thread the longer pointed end of the cut paste through the centre section. This will create a twist effect in the sides of each piece of paste.

~ 2 ~

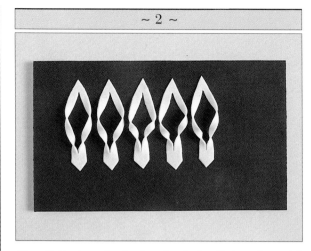

Carefully brush the back of the link twist with sugar glue and secure to the cake. Repeat with the additional link twists, ensuring they are level. Adjust their positions with a dresden tool, then neaten the top edge of each with the blade of the ribbon insertion cutter.

~ 3 ~

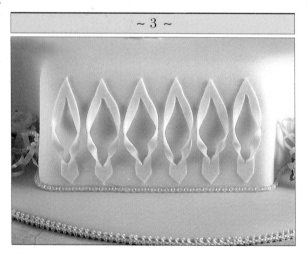

When the sections have dried, take a soft paintbrush and apply a little yellow dusting powder to the twisted paste.

~ 4 ~

Make up five small sprays of flowers, consisting of pale yellow silk roses, loops of ribbon and pearl beading, then secure together with white stem fix. Trim a white posy frill down to 7.5cm(3 in) in diameter and arrange roses, ribbons and pearl beading inside.

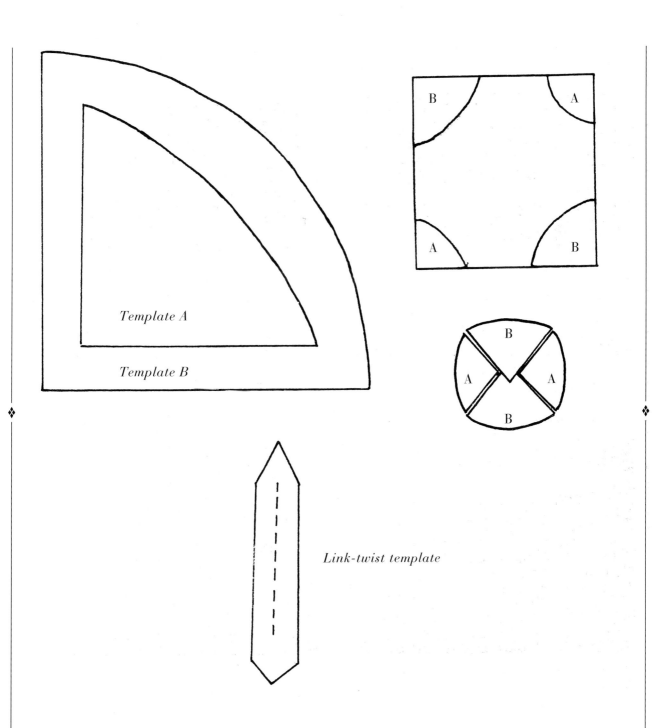

Template A

Template B

Link-twist template

HAPPY 21ST KARINA

20cm(8 in) hexagonal cake
apricot glaze
875g(1¾ lb) marzipan (almond paste)
1.25kg(2½ lb) cream sugarpaste
clear alcohol (gin, vodka, kirsch)
pale green, chestnut brown and lemon yellow
liquid food colourings
small amount of Royal Icing, see page 13
250g(8 oz/½ lb) Frill Paste, see page 17
Sugar Glue, see page 19
chestnut brown, apple green and green lustre
dusting powder (petal dust/blossom tint)
15g(½ oz/4 tsp) semolina or powdered gelatine,
coloured with lemon yellow dusting powder
(petal dust/blossom tint)
white vegetable fat (shortening)
EQUIPMENT
30cm(12 in) hexagonal cake board
shell modelling tool
scriber
2m(2¼ yd) of 3mm(⅛ in) wide lemon ribbon
no. 1 and 2 piping tubes (tips)
small rolling pin and board
basket weave rolling pin
drying board
10cm(4 in) and 5cm(2 in) pastry cutters
small pieces of foam or sponge
medium paintbrush
small daisy cutter and daisy leaf cutter
cocktail sticks (toothpicks)
ball tool
scalpel
small cranked pallette knife
10cm(4 in) of 1cm(½ in) wide cream ribbon
20cm(8 in) of 5mm(¼ in) wide yellow ribbon

● Cover cake with marzipan and cream sugarpaste, see pages 7 and 9. Colour remaining paste pale lemon and cover the board in one piece, see page 10. Place cake on board and emboss board edge with shell modelling tool.

● Scribe side frill template. Secure lemon ribbon around base of cake and pipe scallop just above with a no. 1 piping tube and white royal icing. Roll out about 60g(2 oz) of the frill paste and cut the frill. Apply frill, folding the paste over to make a small cone in centre of design. Secure to side of cake with sugar glue.

● Pipe a broken line above frill with pale green royal icing and no. 1 piping tube. Cut out circle template, place on cake top and pipe broken line to match side. Pipe message on cake.

● To make the straw boater, colour 125g (4 oz/¼ lb) frill paste a straw colour with a very little chestnut brown colouring. Roll out paste to 1.5mm(1/32 in) thick with small rolling pin and then roll over with basket weave rolling pin. Using the larger pastry cutter, cut out a circle. Cut a smaller circle in the centre and remove to dry. Place a small piece of foam or sponge under either side of the larger circle to give a slight curve to the brim of the hat. Cut a strip of paste for the side using the paper template. Turn the smaller circle over and secure the strip upright around the edge with sugar glue.

● Turn the top of the hat the correct way up and position inside the larger circle, securing with a no. 1 piping tube and pale brown royal icing. Allow to dry.

● Brush over with brown dusting powder. Dampen a piece of absorbent kitchen paper and draw this over the surface. This will remove most of the colour but leave darker areas in the basket weave design.

Roll 30g(1 oz) white frill paste thinly, cut out 20 daisies with the daisy cutter and frill the edges with a cocktail stick. Secure two daisies together with sugar glue and gently cup the centre. With a no. 2 piping tube and soft royal icing, pipe a bulb in the centre of each daisy. Sprinkle with coloured semolina or powdered gelatine and when dry turn over to remove excess.

Colour remaining frill paste a pale apple green and roll thinly. Cut out with a daisy leaf cutter, cutting this into 20 smaller leaves with a scalpel. Allow to dry then brush with apple green dusting powder.

Re-roll the remaining pale green frill paste and cut six bows as shown in the step-by-step sequence. When dry brush with green lustre dusting powder.

Secure the ribbons, daisies and leaves on the hat, and the daisies, leaves and bows on the cake, with white royal icing. Place the hat on the cake and complete the cake by trimming the board with lemon ribbon.

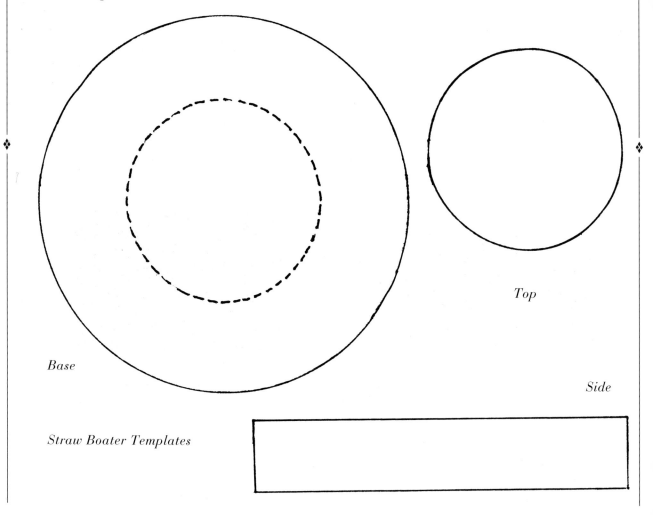

Top

Base

Side

Straw Boater Templates

~ ❖ ~

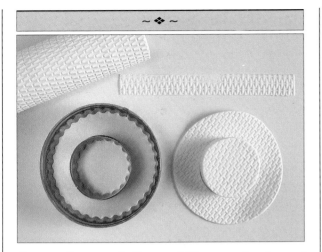

STRAW BOATER *Roll over frill paste firmly and evenly with basket weave rolling pin. Stamp out the two circles and the side of the hat. Place a small piece of foam or sponge under either side of the larger circle and dry. Secure the side to the smaller circle with sugar glue.*

~ ❖ ~

SUGAR LEAVES *Colour the frill paste an apple green and roll thinly. Stamp out with the daisy leaf cutter. Use the scalpel and cut into smaller pieces. Allow to dry then brush with dusting powder.*

~ ❖ ~

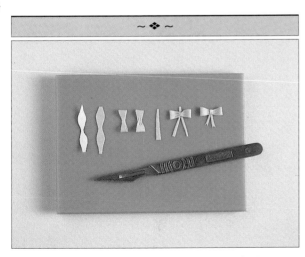

BOWS *Cut out bows in thinly rolled frill paste. Fold ends to centre and secure with sugar glue. Turn over; mark two lines from centre on both sides. Cut tail strip and place bow on it; fold end over and secure with sugar glue. Slit and trim the tail; cut 'V' ends and dry.*

~ ❖ ~

DAISY *Stamp out the daisy. Frill each petal with a cocktail stick. Secure two together with sugar glue, placing the second row of petals in between the first. Cup the centre with a ball tool. Pipe a bulb of royal icing and sprinkle with coloured semolina.*

HAPPY BIRTHDAY

20cm(8 in) scalloped oval cake
apricot glaze
750g(1½ lb) marzipan (almond paste)
1.5kg(3 lb) white sugarpaste
clear alcohol (gin, vodka, kirsch)
small amount of Royal Icing, see page 13
125g(4 oz/¼ lb) Flower Paste, see page 17
ivy green, gooseberry green and peach paste
food colourings
Sugar Glue, see page 19
peach dusting powder (petal dust/blossom tint)
EQUIPMENT
30cm(12 in) thin scalloped oval cake board
10cm(4 in) oval cutter
rose and leaf embossing stamps
no. 1 and 2 piping tubes (tips)
small rolling pin
parsley cutter ● clear acetate film
68 bead-headed pins
20cm(8 in) old, thick cake board
6 cocktail sticks (toothpicks) ● sticky tape
dresden modelling tool
foam or sponge pad
ball tool ● rose calyx cutter
scalpel ● scriber
small cranked palette knife
small paintbrush ● small piece of polystyrene
5 silk rose leaves

Cover the cake with marzipan and 1kg(2 lb) of the white sugarpaste as shown on pages 7 and 9. Allow to dry. Place the cake onto the cake board then, following the instructions on page 13, roll out and apply the drape. Place an oval cutter into position on the drape covering and use gentle pressure to cut through the thin layer of the drape sugarpaste. Remove the cutter then smooth the edges of the cut out shape with your index finger.

Emboss the edge of the drape with the rose and leaf embossers, then pipe small beads with white royal icing, using a no.1 piping tube around the cut edge of the drape, and a no.2 piping tube around the base of the cake.

Make the sugar roses, the quilling plaque and side pieces as described on pages 36 and 37. Scribe the message onto the cake surface then overpipe with peach royal icing, using a no.1 piping tube.

Place the oval quilling plaque over the cut out oval on the cake top, carefully picking it up with a small cranked palette knife, and secure with white royal icing. Pipe dots around the plaque as shown on the template.

Paint the embossed design around the drape with diluted liquid colour. Attach the quilled pieces to the side of the cake with sugar glue. Take a small piece of white sugarpaste and position in the centre of the oval quilling plaque. Place the small quilled piece at the front then gently push the roses and silk leaves into the paste to complete.

EXPERT ADVICE
≈

When quilling, do not roll out the paste too thinly as it will not support the curved shape. It should be just under 1mm(⅟₃₂ in) thick.

To join strips of paste together when making the plaque, open the looped section of paste and insert the end of the new strip. Secure the paste loop together with sugar glue and press the two sides with the dresden tool.

~ 1 ~

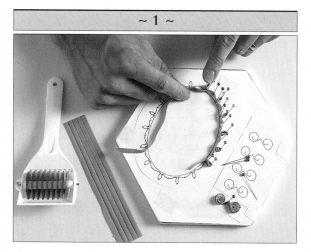

QUILLING Colour 75g(2½ oz) flower paste ivy and gooseberry green. Roll out just under 1mm (¹⁄₃₂ in) thick. Cut with parsley cutter into 20cm(8 in) strips. Place plaque template on an old cake board under acetate film. Position pins and guide the paste over them.

~ 2 ~

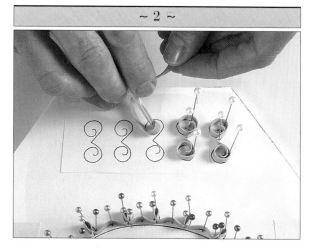

Join two cocktail sticks together with sticky tape. Position over the end of the paste strip and wind the paste around the sticks. Place over the side template, following the pattern, and position the pins. Allow to dry and then carefully remove pins.

~ 1 ~

MOULDED ROSE Form the peach paste into a small cone and then insert a cocktail stick. For each petal take a small ball of paste then flatten with your finger on a rolling board. Use a ball tool to flute the edges and to cup the centre.

~ 2 ~

Position the petals around the cone, applying one, two, three, then five petals, securing to the cone with sugar glue. Allow each layer of petals to dry before applying the next. Apply the calyx then dust the petals with peach dusting powder.

MOULDED ROSE

❖

Knead together 45g(1½ oz) flower paste and 15g(½ oz) sugarpaste and colour the paste pale peach. Mould the cone, inserting a cocktail stick, and allow to dry on a sponge pad, preferably for 12 hours.

For each petal roll a small ball of paste then flatten with your index finger, dusted with a little cornflour to thin the edges. Reform into a petal shape between your thumb and index finger, rolling the edges of the petal with the ball tool to thin and flute.

Apply the first petal to the cone, securing with sugar glue and making sure it wraps tightly around the cone. The next two petals are applied interlocking on opposite sides of the cone. Gently fold over and shape the edges of the petals with your thumb.

The third layer consists of three petals which are applied overlapping, with the last petal tucked inside the first. Allow 30 minutes for each layer to dry before applying the next. The five outer petals are applied in the same way as the previous three, interlocking the last petal under the first.

Roll out ivy and gooseberry green flower paste thinly and cut out the calyx. Make a small cut on each section with a scalpel then roll with a cocktail stick. Secure the calyx to the back of the rose with sugar glue. Stand the cocktail stick (toothpick) in polystyrene until the rose is dry. Dust the edges of the rose when dry with peach dusting powder. Gently twist the cocktail stick to remove the rose and secure to the top of the cake with a small piece of white sugarpaste.

Enlarge by 133% on a photocopier

SILVER WEDDING

20cm(8 in) petal cake
875g(1¾ lb) marzipan (almond paste)
apricot glaze
1.4kg(2¾ lb) white sugarpaste
clear alcohol (gin, vodka, kirsch)
peach paste food colour
small amount of Royal Icing, see page 13
90g(3 oz) Flower Paste, see page 17
cornflour (cornstarch)
peach and silver liquid food colouring
185g(6 oz) Frill Paste, see page 17
Sugar Glue, see page 19
silver sparkle dusting powder (petal
dust/blossom tint)

E Q U I P M E N T

30cm(12 in) thick petal cake board
design and message embossing stamps
no. 1 and 2 piping tubes (tips)
small rolling pin
10cm(4 in) oval cutter
nos. 2 and 5 cutters
medium and small bell moulds
foam or sponge pad
scalpel
dog bone and dresden modelling tools
small cranked palette knife
medium paintbrush
emery board
dried green gypsophila
3 small silk flowers
2m(2¼ yd) of 3mm(⅛ in) wide peach satin
ribbon
1m(1 yd) of 1cm(½ in) wide white satin ribbon

Cover the cake with marzipan and 1kg(2 lb) of the white sugarpaste as shown on pages 7 and 9. Place the cake on the board. Save the sugarpaste trimmings for making the message plaque.

Colour 375g(12 oz/¾ lb) sugarpaste pale peach and cover the board using the strip method shown on page 10. Smooth the two edges together with your fingers then polish with a smoother. Emboss the board edge with the design embossing stamp, as described on page 14. Allow to dry then pipe beads around the base of the cake with a no.1 piping tube and white royal icing . Allow the beads to dry then overpipe the design with an interweaving line of pale peach.

Roll out the flower paste to 1mm(½₂ in) thick then cut out the oval shape with the cutter. Re-roll the paste trimmings thinly, then stamp out the numbers, putting them to dry on a flat surface. Colour the remaining flower paste pale peach and then mould the bells as shown on page 41, taking the paste from the mould, dusting with a little cornflour, then placing back and continuing to shape.

Turn the completed bells out of the moulds and place in an upright position on a piece of foam or sponge. Leave to dry for 12 hours.

Brush a piece of paper with liquid peach colouring, then roll out the reserved white sugarpaste to 1mm(½₂ in) thick. Imprint the message embossing stamp first onto the colour then onto the sugarpaste. Cut out shape with a scalpel and allow to dry. Reserve the sugarpaste trimmings.

Cut out the templates for the swag and the bow. Colour the frill paste pale peach then cut out and shape six of each, following the instructions on pages 41 and 33. Secure to the cake with sugar glue. When dry dust with silver sparkle dusting powder.

Paint the numbers with silver food colouring

and allow to dry. Gently file the edges of the plaque and the bells with the emery board. Place a small piece of sugarpaste into the bells and position the dried gypsophila, silk flowers and peach ribbon loops. Secure the bells and numbers onto the oval plaque with royal icing, removing the excess with a damp paintbrush.

● Roll a small sausage shape of white sugarpaste trimmings and position the embossed wording against this, securing with a little sugar glue to the top of the cake. The bell decoration can be secured to the cake with 2 – 3 small dots of white royal icing, so that it can be removed for a keepsake after the occasion. Trim the board edge with white and peach ribbon to complete the cake.

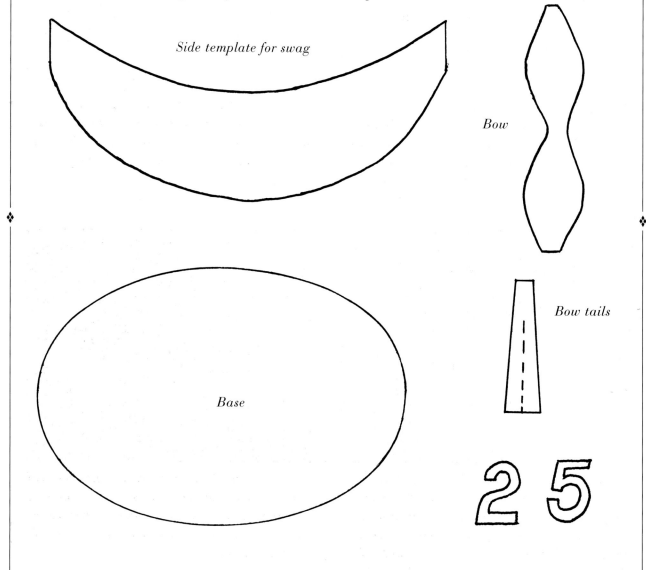

Side template for swag

Bow

Base

Bow tails

~ 1 ~

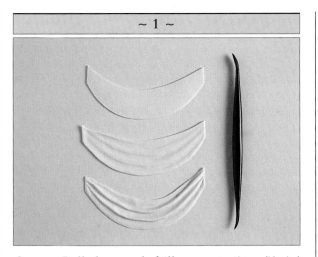

SWAGS Roll the peach frill paste to 1mm(¹⁄₃₂ in) thick. Cut around the swag template. Mark the pleated sections with the dog bone tool, then press the dresden tool onto its side along each pleated section. Pinch the section between thumb and index finger to emphasize the pleat.

~ 2 ~

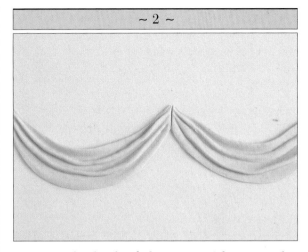

Moisten the back of the swag with sugar glue and position into place on the cake side. Pull the middle section of the swag away from the cake. Use the dresden tool to neaten the joins at the top edge of the swag.

~ 1 ~

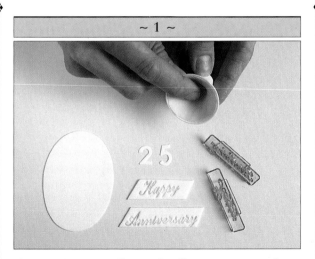

SUGAR BELLS Roll out the flower paste and cut the oval base and numbers. Mould the sugar bells from peach flower paste, lightly dusting the inside of the mould with cornflour (cornstarch). Press paste into mould until thin. Trim the edge of the bells and turn out to dry.

~ 2 ~

Paint the numbers. Arrange the flowers and ribbon inside the bells, using a small piece of sugarpaste. Secure the bells and numbers to the plaque. Dust the bells with silver sparkle dusting powder.

ENGAGEMENT

25cm(10 in) heart-shaped cake
1.25kg(2½ lb) marzipan (almond paste)
apricot glaze
2kg(4 lb) white sugarpaste
clear alcohol (gin, vodka, kirsch)
peach and apple green paste food colours
small amount of Royal Icing, see page 13
250g(8 oz/½ lb) Frill Paste, see page 17
Sugar Glue, see page 19
60g(2 oz) Flower Paste, see page 17
edible glitter

EQUIPMENT

36cm(14 in) thick heart-shaped cake board
heart cutter • dresden modelling tool
small heart plunger cutter • crimper
1m(1 yd) of 3mm(⅛ in) wide peach ribbon
no.1 piping tube (tip)
scriber • curved cutter
leaf eyelet cutter
scalloped endless frill cutter
foam or sponge pad • ball tool
peach food colouring pen (italic)
1m(1 yd) of 1cm(½ in) wide white ribbon

● Cover the cake with marzipan and white sugarpaste, see pages 7 and 9; place on the board. While the paste is soft, cut out the heart shapes on the top, see page 12. Do not cut down into the marzipan. Leaving the cutter in place, use the dresden tool to remove the sugarpaste centre. Allow the paste to dry. Colour the hearts peach and insert them in place, then smooth over the edges.

● Cover the board using the strip method, see page 10, with the join at the back of the heart. Cut out the two hearts on the board with the small plunger cutter, then replace with peach

sugarpaste. Crimp the board edge, see page 14, and leave to dry. Secure peach ribbon around the cake base and pipe beads with a no.1 piping tube and white royal icing.

● Scribe a line 7.5cm(3 in) from the base of the cake. Roll frill paste 1mm(¹⁄₃₂ in) thick and use the curved cutter and the leaf eyelet cutter to cut out side pieces, see page 18. Two adjoining sections can be cut and applied to the scribe line. Start at the front and secure the pieces with sugar glue, then work around the cake side.

● Roll frill paste 1mm (¹⁄₃₂ in) thick and cut out the top section using the scalloped endless frill cutter. Cut two adjoining sections, start at the front and secure above the lower section with sugar glue.

● Roll the peach-coloured flower paste thinly. Cut out 32 small hearts with the plunger cutter, place on a foam pad, cup the centre with a ball tool and allow to dry.

● Tilt the cake slightly away from you and attach four hearts in a flower shape on each side section with white royal icing. Pipe around the eyelet holes with a no.1 piping tube and pale green royal icing. Pipe a small bulb of white royal icing in the centre and six small green dots around the bulb.

● Scribe the curve around the hearts onto the top of the cake. Write the inscription with the food colouring pen. Outline the hearts and pipe the names onto the heart shapes with a no.1 piping tube and pale green royal icing. Pipe over the scribed curve and the inscription. Attach the cut-out hearts on the top.

● Dampen the inlaid hearts and sprinkle with edible glitter. Trim the board edge with ribbon and add a small bow to the cake base.

SPIRAL CELEBRATION CAKE

25cm(10 in) oval cake
apricot glaze
875g(1¾ lb) marzipan (almond paste)
2kg(4 lb) cream sugarpaste
clear alcohol (gin, vodka, kirsch)
apple green, fern green and burgundy paste food colourings
small amount of Royal Icing, see page 13
90g(3 oz) Frill Paste, see page 17
apple green and burgundy dusting powders (petal dust/blossom tint)
15g(½ oz) Flower Paste, see page 17

EQUIPMENT

36cm(14 in) thick oval cake board
no. 1, 2 and 3 piping tubes (tips)
small and medium ivy leaf cutters
ball tool
dresden modelling tool
corrugated plastic sheet
fine and medium soft paintbrushes
3 medium silk chrysanthemums
3 small silk flowers
short length of 3mm(⅛ in) wide burgundy ribbon
1.25m(1⅓ yd) of 1cm(½ in) wide burgundy ribbon

• Cover the cake with marzipan and 1.5kg (3 lb) of the cream sugarpaste, see pages 7 and 9. While still soft, emboss the spiral effect on the top and side, see pages 18 and 69.

• Place the cake off centre onto the board. Marble the remaining sugarpaste with the green food colours as shown on page 24, then cover the board using the strip method shown on page 10. With white royal icing and a no.2 piping tube, pipe beads around the base of the cake. Pipe a small dot between the white beads with pale green royal icing, using a no.1 piping tube.

• Colour the frill paste with apple green and roll out to 1mm(½2 in) thick. Using the cutters, stamp out 15 small and 27 medium ivy leaves. Smooth the edges of the leaves with a ball tool and mark the veins with the dresden tool. Place the leaves onto corrugated plastic sheet to dry. Dust the dry leaves with apple green dusting powder to give a variegated effect, and lightly apply burgundy dusting powder to the edges.

• Cut out the tag from the thinly rolled flower paste, using the paper template as a guide. Cut the small hole in the tag with a no.3 piping tube. Allow to dry. Secure the leaves and flowers to the cake and board with pale green royal icing. Paint the message onto the tag with liquid burgundy colouring and thread the thin ribbon through the hole. Attach the tag to the cake with royal icing. Trim the board with burgundy ribbon to complete the cake.

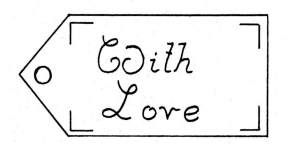

FIRST BIRTHDAY

20cm(8 in) square cake
apricot glaze
1.125kg(2¼ lb) marzipan (almond paste)
1.5kg(3 lb) white sugarpaste
clear alcohol (gin, vodka, kirsch)
pink, black and fern green paste food
colourings
small amount of Royal Icing, see page 13
125g(4 oz/¼ lb) Flower Paste, see page 17
white vegetable fat (shortening)
Sugar Glue, see page 19
15g(½ oz) caster sugar

EQUIPMENT

28cm(11 in) square cake board
crimpers
no. 0, 1 and 2 piping tubes (tips)
scalpel
drying board
plaque cutter
small cranked palette knife
small blossom plunger cutter
foam or sponge pad
ball tool
pink food colouring pen
scriber
fine paintbrush
1.25m(4 ft) of 1cm(½ in) wide silver board
edging

● Cover the cake with marzipan and 1.25kg (2½ lb) white sugarpaste as shown on pages 7 and 9. Place the cake onto the cake board. Colour the remaining sugarpaste pale pink then cover the board using the strip method shown on page 10. While the paste is still soft crimp the edge of the board, observing the instructions for crimper work on page 14. There is no template required for this. Pipe beads around the cake base with white royal icing and a no.2 piping tube.

● Colour the the flower paste pale pink and roll out to 1mm(1⁄32 in) thick. Cut out the collar, see page 48, with a scalpel. Use the larger end of a piping tube to cut out the circles. Place the collars on a drying board and leave for 12 hours, turning occasionally.

● Re-roll the leftover flower paste to 1.5mm (1⁄12 in) thick then cut out the plaque for the base, reserving trimmings. Allow to dry.

● Cut out the bear card paper template then rub a little white vegetable fat onto the back of the template. Roll out the pink flower paste trimmings to 1mm(1⁄32 in) thick, then position the template on the paste and cut out with a scalpel. Mark down the side of the bear on the flower paste with the edge of a small cranked palette knife. Position a piece of folded paper under the bear card, to rest on until dry. Allow to dry for 12 hours.

● Stamp out about 100 small pink blossoms from the leftover, thinly rolled, flower paste. Place the blossoms onto a piece of foam or sponge and cup each centre with the ball tool. Allow to dry.

● Draw around the bear shape on the cut out flower paste card with a pale pink food colouring pen. Scribe the wording on the card and plaque, see page 48.

EXPERT ADVICE

≈

When making blossoms, cut and eject 10 blossoms at a time, then hollow their centres as this speeds up the process.

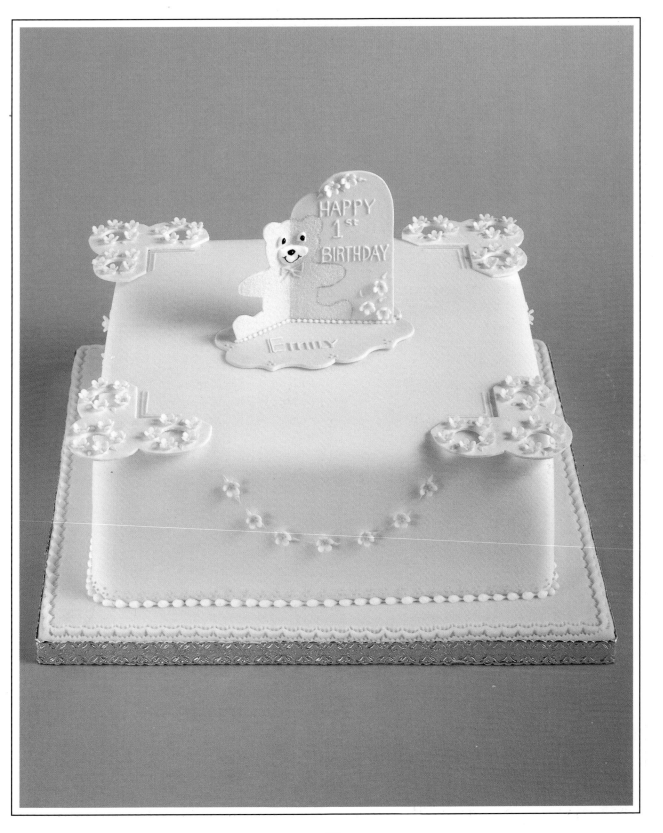

Brush the bear with a little sugar glue then sprinkle over the caster sugar. Pipe the eyes and nose with soft white royal icing then allow to dry. Paint the eyes, nose and mouth with black colour, using a fine paintbrush.

Overpipe the wording with pale green royal icing, using a no.1 piping tube. Pipe a bow with pink royal icing using a no.0 piping tube, then pipe three pink dots inside the blossoms and attach to the card around the wording. Pipe green leaves around the blossoms. Place the card onto the plaque and pipe beads with pale green royal icing around the base of the card to secure. Pipe dots with pink royal icing onto the plaque base and around the cake base, above the beading.

Position the template around the side of the cake and mark the point for each blossom flower. Pipe small green leaves with a no.1 piping tube on either side of these points. Pipe a small bulb of white royal icing between each pair of leaves and attach the blossoms. Pipe three pink dots into the centre of each blossom.

Pipe five bulbs of white royal icing with a no. 2 piping tube around each circle on the collar section, then attach the blossom flowers. Pipe leaves radiating from between each blossom flower with pale green royal icing. Pipe three dots of pink royal icing into each blossom flower. Attach the collar pieces onto the corners of the cake with white royal icing, using a no. 2 piping tube. Pipe a pink and green line inside each of the collar sections on the cake surface to complement the colour scheme. Attach the bear card to the cake with 2 – 3 dots of royal icing, so that it can be removed from the cake for a keepsake. Finally, trim the board with silver edging.

Collar piece

~ 1 ~

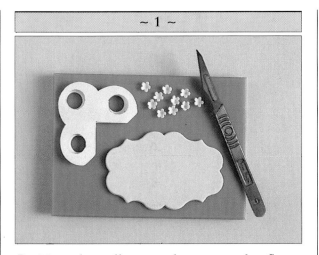

Position the collar template onto the flower paste and cut out four sections with a scalpel. Cut out the plaque base. Cut out the circles with the larger end of a piping tube. Cut out 100 pink blossom flowers and cup their centres with a ball tool.

~ 2 ~

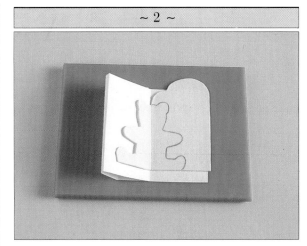

Roll out the pale pink flower paste then cut around the bear card template. Position folded paper under the cut out card and allow to dry. Draw the outline of the bear with a pale pink food colouring pen, then brush the bear with sugar glue and sprinkle over caster sugar.

~ 3 ~

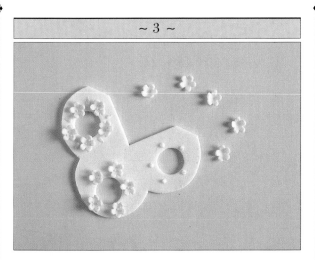

Pipe five bulbs of white royal icing around each circle then attach the blossom flowers. Pipe three pink dots into each blossom then pipe leaves between each flower.

~ 4 ~

Pipe the eyes and nose with white royal icing then allow to dry. Paint on the eyes, nose and mouth with black food colour. Pipe a small bow, and the wording on the card. Attach the blossom flowers and assemble the card onto the plaque with beads of royal icing.

ORIENTAL MAGIC

30cm(12 in) fan-shaped cake
apricot glaze
1.25kg(2½ lb) marzipan (almond paste)
about 2.5kg(5 lb) white sugarpaste
clear alcohol (gin, vodka, kirsch)
fuchsia pink and lemon paste food colours
Sugar Glue, see page 19
small amount of Royal Icing, see page 13
yellow and pink dusting powder (petal
dust/blossom tint)

EQUIPMENT

48cm(19 in) thin fan-shaped cake board
2m(2¼ yd) of 1cm(½ in) wide yellow ribbon
2m(2¼ yd) of 5mm(¼ in) wide pink ribbon
no. 1 and 2 piping tubes (tips)
cranked palette knife
scriber
flower nail
small angled scissors
dresden modelling tool
umbrella modelling tool
soft medium paintbrush
2m(2¼ yd) of 5mm(¼ in) wide yellow ribbon

This cake can be adapted for any occasion. The use of the sugarpaste to create the flowers makes them completely edible! Experiment with different colours of sugarpaste to make the chrysanthemums, the result is effective and simple to achieve.

Cover the cake with marzipan and 1.4kg (2¾ lb) white sugarpaste as shown on page 7 and 9. Colour 125g(4 oz/¼ lb) each of sugarpaste a pale pink and lemon, then roll together with 625g(1¼ lb) of white sugarpaste to create the marble effect as shown on page 24. Cover the board in one piece as shown on page 10.

Place the cake onto the cake board. Secure the wide yellow and thin pink ribbons around the cake with sugar glue. Hold in place with pins until set then remove. Place small bows over the joins of the ribbon. Pipe beads around the base of the cake with a no.2 piping tube and yellow royal icing. Overpipe with pink royal icing using a no.1 piping tube.

Roll out 250g(8 oz/½ lb) white sugarpaste, and cut out the fan pieces using the paper template. Mark the lines with the edge of a cranked palette knife and cut out the circle with the larger end of a piping tube. Place onto the cake surface to dry, then secure with sugar glue. Scribe over the design then pipe with yellow royal icing using a no.1 piping tube. Pipe the small dots onto the fan with soft pink royal icing, using a no.1 piping tube. Make the flowers as shown on page 52 then position onto the cake, securing with royal icing. Pipe small pink dots and a few white petals around the flowers on the board, using a no. 1 piping tube. Trim the board edge with yellow ribbon.

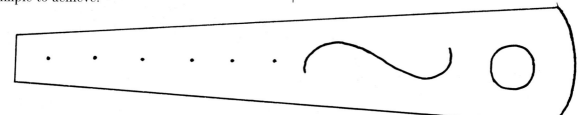

~ 1 ~

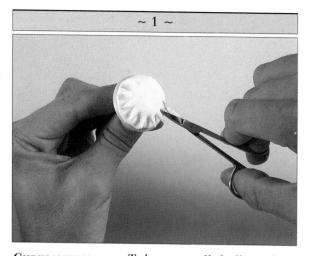

CHRYSANTHEMUMS *Take a small ball each of lemon and white sugarpaste trimmings. Place the white sugarpaste uppermost onto a flower nail. Take a pair of angled scissors and make about 15 cuts, pressing the scissors down into the paste as you cut.*

~ 2 ~

Cut with the scissors under the first row of petals. Remove the surplus paste from around the base of the flower with a dresden tool. Mark the centre of each lower petal with the dresden tool.

~ 3 ~

Cut a third row of petals between the top petals (about 13 cuts). Mark the petals on each row with the dresden tool. Cut the fourth row of petals (about nine cuts). Mark the centre with an umbrella tool and then make six cuts around the centre.

~ 4 ~

Remove the flower with a cranked palette knife and place onto a small ball of sugarpaste so that it can open out. Allow to dry then dust the petal edges with yellow and pink dusting powder. Secure to the cake top and cake board with white royal icing.

DINOSAUR

20cm(8 in) long octagonal cake
1.6kg(3¼ lb) white sugarpaste
chestnut brown, green, orange, mauve, red
and black food colourings
apricot glaze
750g(1½ lb) marzipan (almond paste)
clear alcohol (gin, vodka, kirsch)
Sugar Glue, see page 19
small amount of Royal Icing, see page 13
clear confectioners' glaze

EQUIPMENT

33cm(13 in) long thick octagonal cake board
1cm(½ in) round cutter
50cm(½ yd) of 2.5cm(1 in) wide orange ribbon
ribbed rolling pin
scriber
no. 1 piping tube (tip)
dresden modelling tool
ball tool
small sharp knife
fine and medium paintbrushes
1m(1 yd) of 1cm(½ in) wide orange ribbon
1m(1 yd) mauve sequin waste
non-toxic glue

Colour 875g(1¾ lb) of the sugarpaste pale chestnut brown, then cover the cake with marzipan and sugarpaste as shown on pages 7 and 9. Allow to dry. Colour 625g(1¼ lb) sugarpaste green and cover the board in one piece as shown on page 10. Position the cake onto the board. Cut out the small circles on the board with the cutter, and replace with orange sugarpaste circles. Further instructions for inlay work can be found on pages 12 and 13.

Measure and cut a band of parchment the circumference of the cake, then fold into 14 pieces. Cut a triangle, see page 67, adjusting the template so it is the same size as one of the folded sections. Secure the orange ribbon to the cake with sugar glue. Roll the remaining green paste 1.5mm(½ in) thick, then cut out the circles of paste at regular intervals with the small round cutter - the circles should be sufficiently far apart for the triangle template to be fitted between them. Replace with orange cut out circles. Roll over the paste with the ribbed rolling pin.

Place the triangle template on the paste, with the orange circle in the middle and cut around it. Cut out a further 13 triangles with orange circles in the middle. Secure the triangles to the cake with sugar glue. Cut the top piece using the paper template, then cut out circles and replace with orange paste as for the triangles. Colour a little sugarpaste mauve and cut 12 circles, placing them on the cake side between the triangles, but not in the spaces occupied by the ribbon. Scribe the message onto the cake top then pipe over with dark mauve royal icing and a no.1 piping tube. Pipe the design around the base.

Colour 52g(1¾ oz) sugarpaste purple, 45g (1½ oz) pale green, a small piece red, and a small piece orange. Shape the pieces to form the dinosaur, using the template as a guide, then follow the instructions on page 54.

Add the feet, tongue and spots, painting on the eyes when dry with black food colour. Paint the dinosaur with confectioners' glaze when dry. Position the dinosaur onto the cake and secure with a little sugar glue. Trim the board edge with the orange ribbon and the sequin waste.

~ 1 ~

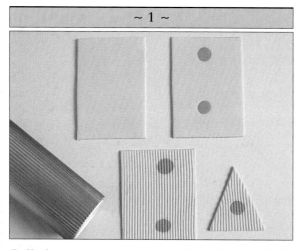

Roll the green sugarpaste 1.5mm(⅟₁₂ in) thick. Cut out circles with the small round cutter. Replace orange sugarpaste circles into the holes. Roll over the paste with a ribbed rolling pin, then cut out the shapes using the template.

~ 2 ~

Use the palms of your hands to shape the sugarpaste. Place the two body sections together. Mark on the lines with the dresden tool. Hollow the eyes with the ball tool and cut the mouth with a small sharp knife. Secure the sections together with sugar glue.

HAVE

A ROARING

TIME

ASHLEY!

Design on board edge

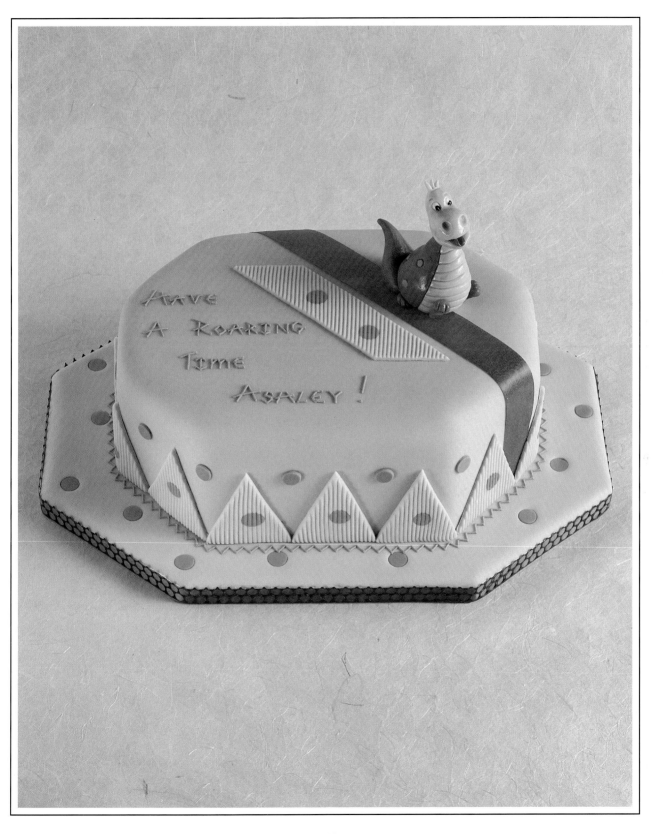

LAURA

20cm(8 in) oval cake
apricot glaze
750g(1½ lb) marzipan (almond paste)
875g(1¾ lb) white sugarpaste
clear alcohol (gin, vodka, kirsch)
Sugar Glue, see page 19
small amount of Royal Icing, see page 13
60g(2 oz) Flower Paste, see page 17
pink, mauve and chestnut brown paste
food colourings
pearl and mauve iridescent food colourings
E Q U I P M E N T
30cm(12 in) thin oval cake board
masking tape
5mm(¼ in) plain crimper
1m(1yd) of 3mm(⅛ in) wide pale pink ribbon
2m(2¼ yd) of 3mm(⅛ in) wide light
mauve ribbon
no. 1 piping tube (tip)
ballet dancer mould
small cranked palette knife
scalpel
medium and fine paintbrushes
2 cocktail sticks (toothpicks)

● Follow stages for covering cake with marzipan and sugarpaste shown on pages 7 and 9. Reserve the sugarpaste trimmings. While paste is still soft measure the circumference of the cake with a band of parchment. Fold in half, then in half again; draw around a pastry cutter on the parchment to make the curve template to follow for the crimper work. Cut out, then secure around the cake with masking tape, ensuring the design is even. Place the cake on a turntable, tilted slightly away from you, and crimp the paste using the template as your guide (see page 14). Allow paste to dry and place the cake onto the cake board.

● Secure pink and mauve ribbons with sugar glue around base of cake, leaving 5mm(¼ in) gap and joining at the front. Make two small bows then attach to the ribbon over the joins. Pipe white beads around base of cake with white royal icing, using a no. 1 piping tube.

● Knead the sugarpaste trimmings with the flower paste, to make frill paste. Mould the ballet dancer, as shown on page 20 and 21, and paint on details. Cut out the paste for garlands, see page 12, and secure a strip each of mauve and pink with sugar glue, following the scalloped shape of the crimping. Make the garlands, then secure them to the cake with sugar glue, as shown on page 12. Twist the two colours of paste together and roll thinly.

● Cut lengths of the two-coloured rolled paste and form into the required name and number. Stick overlapping pieces together with sugar glue. When dry secure to the cake top with sugar glue, then secure the ballet dancer into place and arrange small diamond pieces around her. Attach garlands to her hands. Finally trim the board edge with light mauve ribbon.

HAPPY RETIREMENT

25cm(10 in) diamond-shaped cake
apricot glaze
750g(1½ lb) marzipan (almond paste)
1.25kg(2½ lb) white sugarpaste
pink and lilac food paste colourings
clear alcohol (gin, vodka, kirsch)
small amount of Royal Icing, see page 13
125g(4 oz/¼ lb) Frill Paste, see page 17
185g(6 oz) Smocking Paste, see page 19
Sugar Glue, see page 18

EQUIPMENT

45cm(18 in) long, thick, diamond-shaped cake
board
no. 1 piping tube (tip)
scriber
lace cutter with small heart insert
ribbed rolling pin
endless frill cutter
tweezers
small cranked pallette knife
3 silk anemone flowers
5 silk anemone leaves
1.25m(4 ft) of 1cm(½ in) wide white ribbon
1.25m(4 ft) of 5mm(¼ in) wide pale lilac ribbon

Cover the cake with marzipan as shown on page 7. Colour the sugarpaste very pale pink and cover the cake as shown on page 9. Add lilac colour to the pale pink sugarpaste then cover the board using the one-piece method described on page 10. Allow to dry. Place the cake onto the board and pipe beads around the base with a no.1 piping tube and white royal icing.

Scribe lines with the scriber and a ruler for the top lace piece and the side smocking. Follow instructions on pages 18 and 19 and apply the lace and smocking to the cake. Scribe the message and the board design as shown on page 10 then overpipe with dark lilac royal icing, using a no.1 piping tube.

Position a small ball of sugarpaste onto the cake and push the silk flowers and leaves into the paste. Trim the board edge with the ribbons to complete.

Piped design on board

Happy
Retirement

COUNTRY WEDDING

15cm(6 in) scalloped oval cake
20cm (8 in) scalloped oval cake
apricot glaze
1.25kg(2½ lb) marzipan (almond paste)
2.25kg(4½ lb) white sugarpaste
clear alcohol (gin, vodka, kirsch)
Frill Paste, see page 17
pink, lemon, blue and brown food paste
colourings
Sugar Glue, see page 19
small amount of Royal Icing, see page 13
pink and silver sparkle dusting powder (petal
dust/blossom tint)
155 g (5 oz) Flower Paste see page 17
food colouring pens

EQUIPMENT

20cm(8 in) thin scalloped oval cake board
36cm(14 in) thin scalloped oval cake board
endless frill cutter with small scalloped insert
single eyelet cutter
no.1 piping tube (tip)
scriber
large, medium and small rose petal cutters
small blossom plunger cutter
ball tool
scalpel
small round cutter
small heart plunger cutter
drying board
fine and medium paintbrushes
palette for mixing colours
small pieces of foam or sponge
foam or sponge pad
3 perspex (plexiglass) barley twist cake pillars
short lengths of 3mm(⅛ in) wide pink and
white ribbon

Cover the cakes with marzipan and sugarpaste, as shown on pages 7 and 9, then place onto the cake boards to dry.

Colour one third of the frill paste pale pink. Roll thinly then, with the endless frill cutter, cut four separate sections for each scallop of the cake. Use the single eyelet cutter to cut out the inserts. Secure to the base of the cakes with sugar glue. Pipe beads around the base of each cake with white royal icing and a no.1 piping tube.

Roll the remaining frill paste and cut out the top frill with the cutter set wider, observing the technique for frilling shown on page 16. Colour the edge of the frill with pink dusting powder when dry. Pipe the design above the top frill, and the small dots below the frill using a no.1 piping tube and white royal icing.

Make the carriage and horseshoes as shown on pages 62 and 63. Secure the horseshoes to the cake, with a little royal icing, holding in position with small pieces of sponge until set. Paint the detail on the carriage then assemble as shown on page 63. Place the top cake in position supported on three perspex pillars. Secure the top decoration to the cake with a little royal icing, so it can be easily removed for a keepsake after the occasion.

NOTE You can cut out a special numberplate for the carriage, if you like, or even attach a 'Just Married' sign to it.

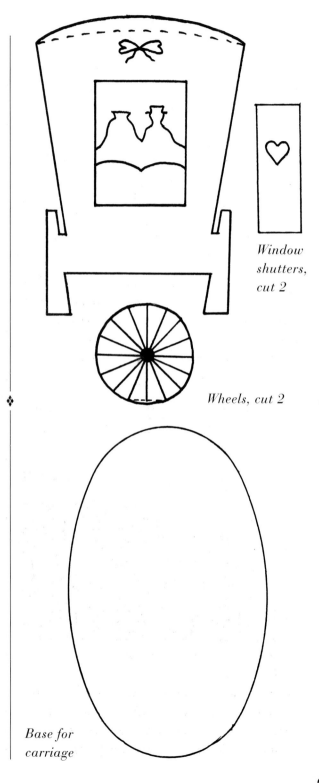

Window shutters, cut 2

Wheels, cut 2

Base for carriage

~ 1 ~

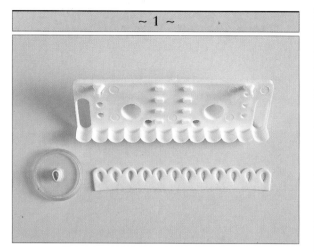

Colour one third of the frill paste pale pink and roll out thinly. Cut the scalloped lace, using the single eyelet cutter to cut out the insert. Secure to the cake with sugar glue.

~ 4 ~

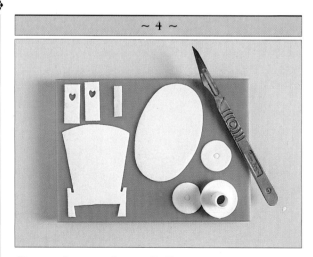

Trace the templates. Roll out remaining paste to 1mm($\frac{1}{32}$ in) thick. Cut out the carriage with a scalpel. Cut the wheels with a round cutter. Cut out the shutters and plaque base, making the windows in the shutters with the small heart plunger cutter. Leave to dry for 12 hours.

~ 2 ~

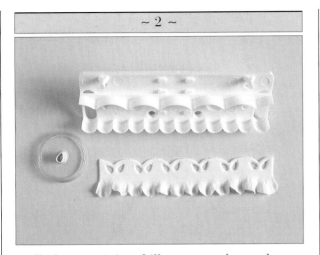

Roll the remaining frill paste and cut the top frill, observing the technique for frilling on page 16. Scribe a line about 7.5cm (3 in) from the cake base around the top edge of the side of the cake. Secure the top frill onto the scribed line with sugar glue.

~ 3 ~

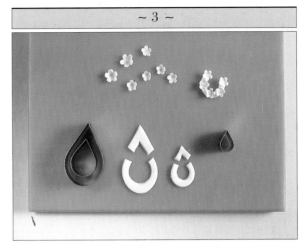

Roll out about 45g (1½ oz) white flower paste to 1mm (¹⁄₃₂ in) thick. Use rose petal cutters to make horseshoes. Stamp out pale pink, yellow and blue small blossoms; cup each centre with the ball tool. Apply blossoms to horseshoes with royal icing and dry.

~ 5 ~

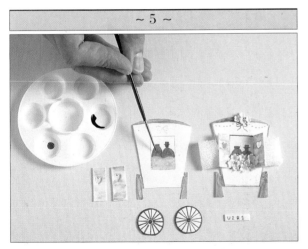

Use diluted food colours or food colouring pens. Shade the carriage, wheels and window shutters. Trace the outline of the bride and groom onto parchment, reverse and transfer onto the carriage. Secure shutters with royal icing and support with sponge until dry.

~ 6 ~

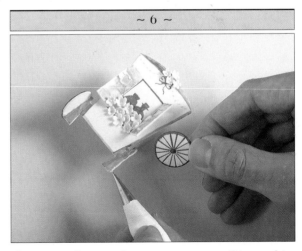

Support the carriage on sponge. Pipe white royal icing with a no. 1 tube to secure the pieces. Stick both wheels onto the side of the carriage and dry. Stand the carriage on the base. Attach the blossoms and ribbons and brush base with silver sparkle dusting powder.

BEST WISHES

25cm(10 in) medium trefoil cake
apricot glaze
1.125kg (2¼ lb) marzipan (almond paste)
2kg(4 lb) white sugarpaste
clear alcohol (gin, vodka, kirsch)
small amount of Royal Icing, see page 13
Sugar Glue, see page 19
green and cyclamen paste food colourings
white vegetable fat (shortening)
60g(2 oz) Flower Paste, see page 17
15g(½ oz) green-coloured semolina
185g(6 oz) Frill Paste, see page 17

EQUIPMENT
33cm(13 in) thick round cake board
dresden modelling tool
scriber
no. 0, 1 and 2 piping tubes (tips)
1m(1 yd) of 5mm(¼ in) wide green ribbon
2 pieces of perspex (plexiglass)
7.5cm(3 in) oval cutter
medium paintbrush
clear acetate film
small cranked palette knife
foam or sponge pad
medium blossom cutter
ball tool
scalpel
endless frill cutter
1m(1 yd) of 1cm(½ in) wide silver board edging

Cover the cake with marzipan and 1.5kg (3 lb) of the sugarpaste as shown on pages 7 and 9. Place the cake onto the board and then cover the board with the remaining sugarpaste, using the strip method shown on page 10. While the paste is still soft, mark on the lines with the dresden tool, radiating from the edge of the cake to the board edge. Allow the sugarpaste to dry.

Scribe the side of the cake with the template as shown on page 10. With white royal icing and a no. 2 piping tube, pipe beads around the base of the cake. Apply the green ribbon just above the piping, securing with sugar glue, and place a bow over the join.

Make the embossed design following the instructions on page 15. Pipe 60 lace pieces with a no. 1 or no. 0 piping tube, see page 20. Make three blossom flowers and five leaves, using the flower paste and following the instructions on pages 20 and 21, and the templates on page 71.

Roll out the frill paste and cut with the endless frill cutter. Apply the flounce, see page 24, along the scribed line, cutting each section to approximate length before securing to the cake with sugar glue. Turn the edges of the flounce under at the ends, leaving enough space to insert the plaque. Pipe beads along the top of the flounce using a no. 1 piping tube and white royal icing. Scribe the inscription onto the cake then use a no.1 piping tube with cyclamen royal icing to pipe over the message.

Secure the plaque, blossoms and leaves onto the cake top with royal icing. Secure the plaque to the side of the cake and attach the lace pieces around the edge and around the top plaque as shown on page 20. Finally trim the board edge with ribbon.

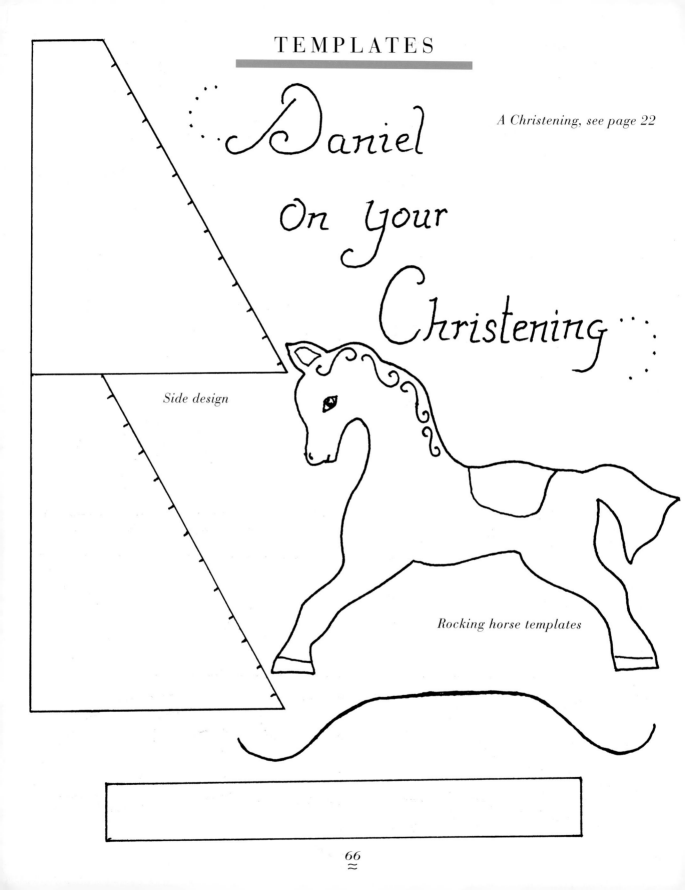

A Christening, see page 22

Daniel On Your Christening

Side design

Rocking horse templates

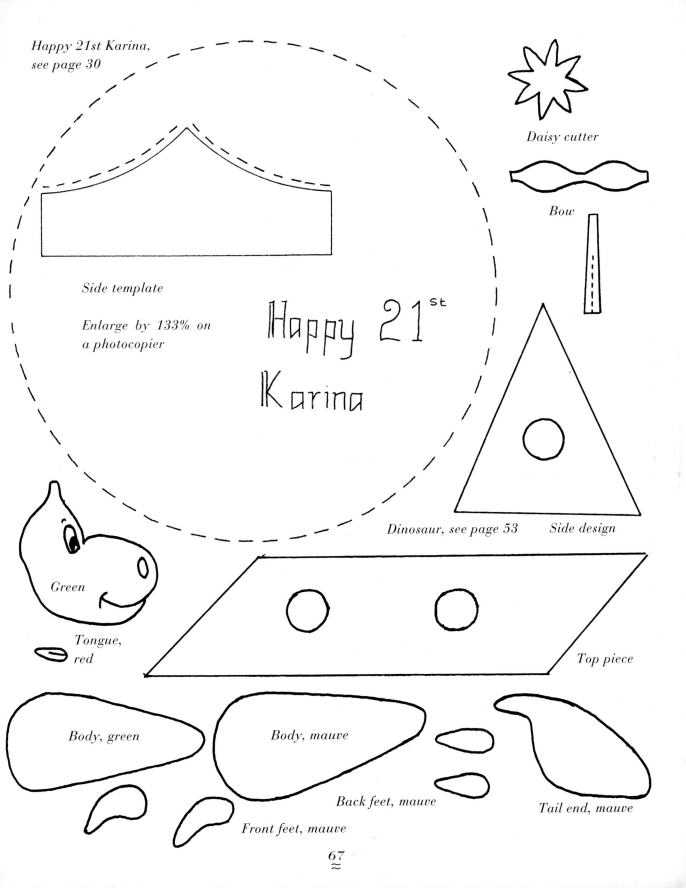

Happy 21st Karina,
see page 30

Daisy cutter

Bow

Side template

Enlarge by 133% on
a photocopier

Happy 21ˢᵗ
Karina

Dinosaur, see page 53   *Side design*

Green

Tongue,
red

Top piece

Body, green   *Body, mauve*

Back feet, mauve

Front feet, mauve   *Tail end, mauve*

Engagement, see page 42

Congratulations On Your Engagement

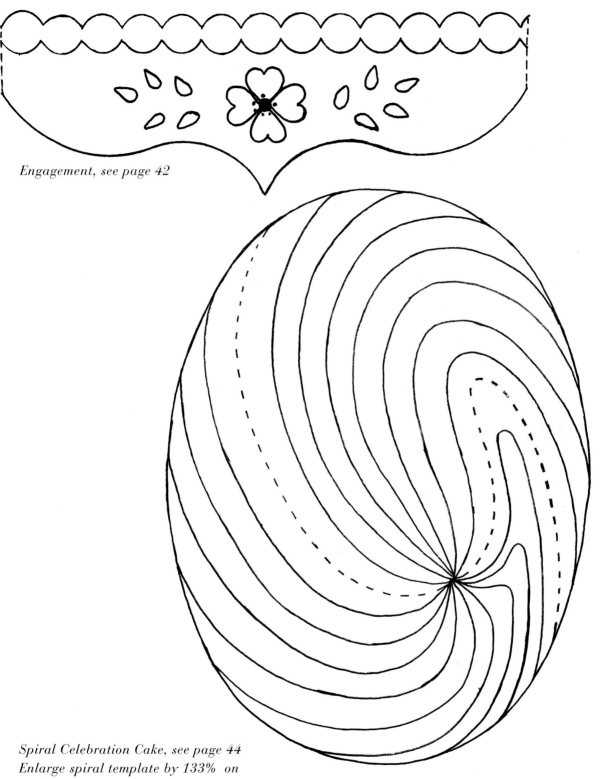

Engagement, see page 42

Spiral Celebration Cake, see page 44
Enlarge spiral template by 133% on
a photocopier

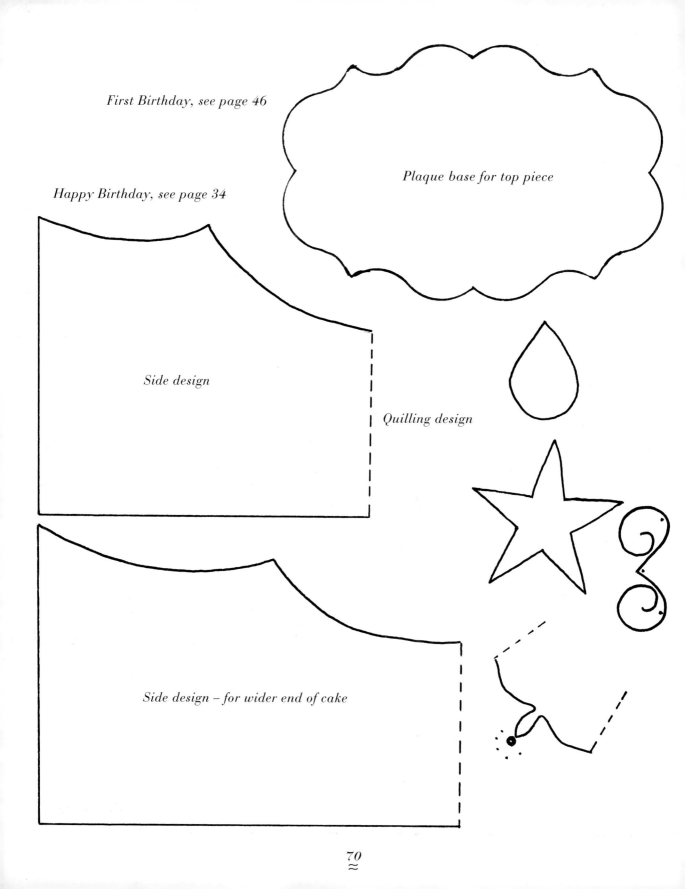

First Birthday, see page 46

Happy Birthday, see page 34

Plaque base for top piece

Side design

Quilling design

Side design – for wider end of cake

First Birthday, see page 46

Side and top template

Blossom flower

Leaf template

Lace

BEST

WISHES

Side design

Best Wishes, see page 64

INDEX

FOR FURTHER INFORMATION

Merehurst is the leading publisher of cake decorating books and has an excellent range of titles to suit cake decorators of all levels. Please send for a free catalogue, stating the title of this book:

United Kingdom
Marketing Department
Merehurst Ltd.
Ferry House
51 -57 Lacy Road
London SW15 1PR
Tel: 081 780 1177
Fax: 081 780 1714

U.S.A./Canada
Foxwood International Ltd.
P.O. Box 267
145 Queen Street S.
Missisauga, Ontario
L5M 2BS Canada
Tel: (1) 416 567 4800
Fax: (1) 416 567 4681

Australia
J.B. Fairfax Ltd.
80 McLachlan Avenue
Rushcutters Bay
NSW 2011
Tel: (61) 2 361 6366
Fax: (61) 2 360 6262

Other Territories
For further information contact:
International Sales Department at United Kingdom address.